Published in 2002 by Caxton Editions
20 Bloomsbury Street
London WC1B 3JH
a member of the Caxton Publishing Group

© 2002 Caxton Publishing Group

Designed and produced for Caxton Editions
by Open Door Limited
Langham, Rutland, UK
Editing: Vanessa Morgan
Typesetting: Jane and Richard Booth
Colour separation: GA Graphics, Stamford, UK

Title: Ultimate Seafood
ISBN: 1 84067 241 2

ULTIMATE

SEAFOOD

For Healthy Living

BRIDGET JONES

CAXTON EDITIONS

4 CONTENTS

6 FANTASTIC SEAFOOD:
THE BENEFITS OF FISH

Seafood is just right for today's healthy lifestyle. For special meals or everyday eating, it is hassle-free and full of goodness – the right, light main ingredient to complement satisfying starchy foods and glorious fruit and vegetables. Fish and shellfish are valuable, low-fat protein foods and are extremely popular for their acknowledged health benefits, particularly for maintaining a healthy weight and helping to avoid heart problems. While white fish is a low-fat source of protein, equivalent in food value to that found in meat, additionally, oily fish provides the omega-3 type of fat that we need in our diets for its positive contribution to health. Fish and seafood also provide useful vitamins and minerals.

Protein for Growth and Repair

The current main focus of advice on the need for eating plenty of fruit and vegetables addresses the problem of diets that contain too much fat and protein on a daily basis. Highly processed meat and poultry products; fat-rich ready meals that are short on vitamin food value; high-fat coatings; and fatty fried foods are all examples of items that are sometimes consumed in too high a quantity and/or too often. However, protein is essential in the diet in modest quantities and it should be prepared and cooked, on the majority of occasions, by methods that are not rich in added fat.

Fish, poultry and meat are the main animal protein foods, while eggs, cheese and milk are dairy sources. Protein is used for building and repairing the body and it should be eaten daily but neither in large quantities nor as the main focus for every meal; indeed, Western diets tend to contain too much protein. Proteins are made up of amino acids, eight of which have to be obtained by adults from food and nine or ten are essential in children's diets. Animal protein provides all of these essential amino acids.

Plant foods also provide protein but they do not include all the essential amino acids in any one food. Soya beans are the exception as they are a source of high-quality protein, equivalent to that of animal sources. Other beans and pulses, rice and grains provide protein. To obtain all the amino acids the body requires from plant sources, a good mix of vegetable foods, including pulses and grains, must be eaten.

In practice, an excellent, non-vegetarian mixed diet will include protein from animal and plant sources, with meat and poultry featuring on some, but not all, days. Fish should be included regularly several times a week, as an alternative to meat or poultry, as well as for the other nutritional benefits it provides.

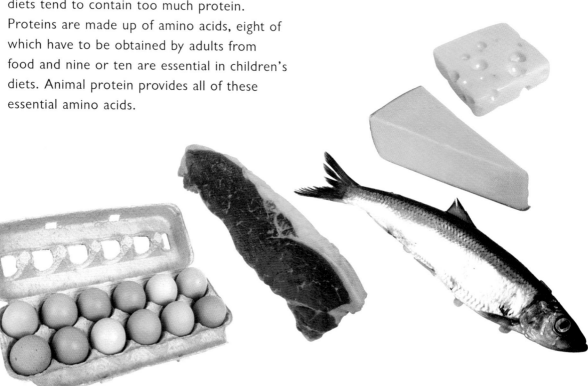

The Good Fats

Fat is also an important nutrient that should not be avoided completely – the idea of a fat-free diet is not a sensible one. The problem with fat and fat-rich foods is that they are particularly palatable and they make the leaner, lighter ingredients taste especially good. What is more, they can be eaten in larger quantities than plain starchy foods and it is easy to develop the habit of eating, and the taste for, a high-fat diet. The answer is in reducing the amount of fat eaten regularly to a small amount so that 'treat' meals taste special with a comparatively modest increase in fat content.

Fats are grouped as saturated or unsaturated, according to their chemical composition. The unsaturated fats may be further divided into polyunsaturated or mono-unsaturated. Animal fats tend to have a higher content of saturated fat than vegetable fats (although there are exceptions to this: coconut and palm oils have high saturated fat contents). The body uses fat as a source and means of storing energy; it is essential in the diet in small amounts. Fat is also important for manufacturing the phospholipids found in cell membranes throughout the body and for growth and general health. The body can manufacture the majority of the fatty acids, which make up the different types of fat, with two notable, important exceptions.

Referred to as essential fatty acids, omega-6 and omega-3 polyunsaturated fatty acids have to be obtained from the diet. Omega-6 fatty acids are found in vegetable oils, such as sunflower and olive oils. Omega-3 fatty acids are found in oily fish as well as vegetable oils and nuts.

Omega-3 fatty acids, the type of fat found in oily fish, have aroused particular interest in recent decades. From many significant studies, it has been established that the omega-3 fatty acids found in oily fish, such as mackerel, salmon and herring, are valuable in preventing heart disease by helping to reduce the likelihood of blood clots, reduce blood pressure and promote healthy heart function.

Vital Vitamins and Minerals

Oily fish are a good source of vitamins A and D. Vitamin A is known for its role in promoting healthy eyes and good sight; it also plays an important part in maintaining the skin and respiratory systems. Vitamin D is important for calcium absorption to promote the development and maintenance of healthy bones and teeth. Fish and seafood are also useful sources of B vitamins, important for a healthy nervous system as well as for converting digested food into energy that can be used by the body.

Fish and seafood provide iodine, selenium, flourine and calcium. Calcium is found in the bones of fish, so it is only available in the diet from the fish that are eaten with their bones – whitebait and herring are good examples. Zinc is also found in seafood, especially oysters and other molluscs.

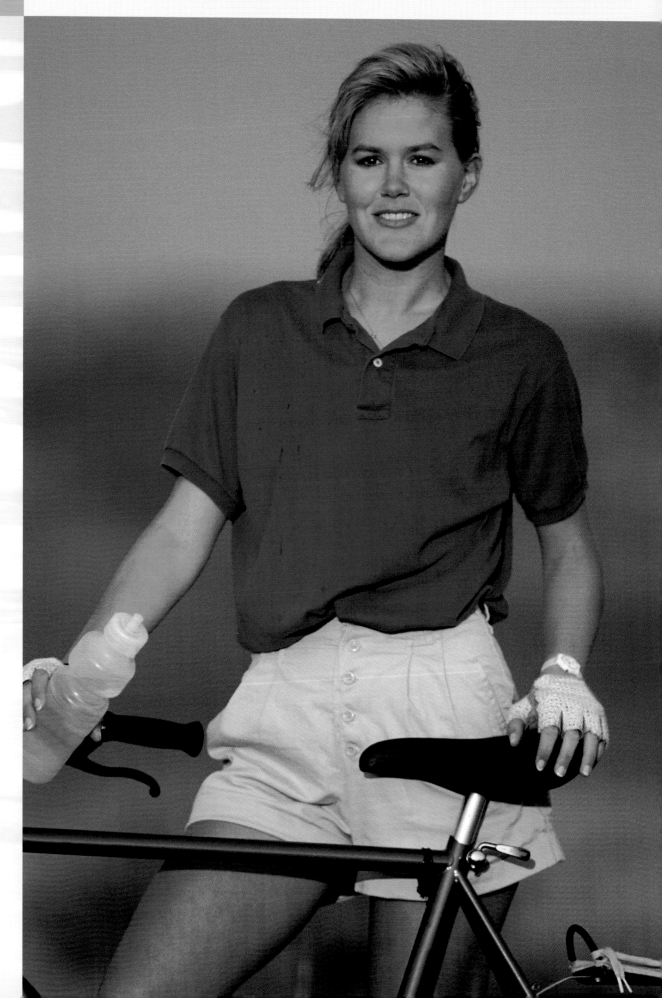

Eating for Wellbeing

The real value of a good diet and its total influence on every aspect of physical health is just being explored and acknowledged. And the contribution food makes to our overall sense of well being is also under scrutiny. In addition to the basic necessity for nutrition to support life, growth and health, the protective and healing properties of simple foods are being discovered – or, perhaps, rediscovered is the appropriate turn of phrase, given that food and herbal remedies were used for generations before modern cures evolved through advances in science.

Why is there such a surge of interest in the broader benefits of diet beyond basic nutrition? During the second half of the twentieth century, eating habits changed dramatically. Highly processed convenience foods have become accepted as everyday meals, too often to the extent that simple ingredients are ignored. Whole generations of young children are growing up on manufactured foods rather than home-cooked items – pizzas; pies; extruded, shaped and coated fish, poultry, meat and vegetables; high-fat snacks; and high-sugar cereals and desserts are just a few examples of items that are eaten frequently by some. The basic ingredients are often extensively processed to create products that have come to be thought of as visually appealing, sometimes with the addition of flavouring and colouring that mask the basic foodstuff completely. The appeal of cheap novelty foods is beginning to be questioned as their true value and, worse, their possible negative influence on good health and development come under scrutiny.

As part of a balanced diet, fish and seafood can help to promote excellent health, protect the body and combat some problems that respond to good eating. Fish and seafood are light and easily digested, and therefore excellent food for people of all ages and constitutions. Poached or boiled fish is an old-fashioned menu for invalids; these days, cooked by simple, appealing contemporary methods it still makes a soothing and easy meal to tempt the weak to eat when the appetite it poor. However, the important contemporary message is that fish is a valuable food for life-long heath and good living. From weaning through to advanced years, fish and seafood can promote physical and mental health by helping to control body weight as part of a calorie-controlled diet, maintaining strong blood circulation, encouraging good skin, keeping joints 'well oiled', and having a positive influence on brain development and function.

A Healthy Cardiovascular System

The link between heart disease and lifestyle is acknowledged and subject to recommendations from health professionals at all levels. We have evolved into a more sedentary society with the problem of overeating and obesity replacing that of starvation and malnutrition through forced lack of food. Moving away from pure ingredients and abandoning simple cooking methods has not helped. Poor cardiovascular health is a problem that can be eased by good eating and some exercise.

Blood is pumped around the body through arteries and it returns to the heart through veins. Circulatory problems occur when cholesterol deposits build up on the inside of the blood vessels, rather like the way in which water pipes fur up with deposits from hard water. When blood vessels are lined with deposits, there is less room for the blood to circulate and more likelihood of clots forming.

Cholesterol is not a plant substance but it is a lipid found exclusively in animal foods. The body manufactures and stores it as an essential substance. Dietary cholesterol is obtained from fat-rich animal foods, such as meat and egg yolks. In the right amounts, cholesterol is not a problem but when the body manufactures too much for its own good and the diet is also a rich source, then it becomes a problem.

Comparisons of different cultures indicate that those consuming diets rich in fish have less heart disease. The Japanese, Portuguese and Spanish are good examples. However, it was studies of Inuit (Eskimo) communities some thirty years ago that first highlighted the possible benefits of a diet rich in omega-3 fatty acids. In spite of their high-fat, cholesterol-rich diets these people displayed low incidence of heart disease and a possible link was made with their diets being extremely rich in omega-3 fatty acids. Continued research of those eating typical Western diets supports the fact that omega-3 fatty acids help to reduce the presence of unwanted fats that encourage blood clotting. They assist in thinning the blood to promote good circulation and reduce the chances of unwanted clotting within the system. This all adds up to improved circulatory health.

Brain Power

Folklore has long associated eating fish with becoming brainy, but now scientific research is beginning to supporting the old-wives' tales. Research into the influence of diet on brain function is in comparative infancy. The brain, the cells of which are formed during pregnancy and early in life, contains a high proportion of fat, with a large percentage of omega-6 and omega-3 fatty acids. Eating a diet rich in oily fish before and during pregnancy may help to promote good brain health in the growing baby. These fatty acids are found in the mother's breast milk, so including oily fish in the diet while breast feeding is also important.

Once again, it is the omega-3 fatty acids that seem to contribute to improved brain function. Not only is this important in terms of child nutrition but there is also the possibility that a diet rich in oily fish can help in the treatment of adult brain-related disorders and problems, such as depression, aggression and schizophrenia. Some studies indicate that depression is not common in those who eat fish regularly and blood levels of omega-3 fatty acids in patients suffering from brain disorders indicate that symptoms are reduced when omega-3 fatty acid levels are increased. Early studies indicate that low levels of omega-3 fatty acids are found in patients suffering from schizophrenia and that taking fish oil supplements helps to reduce the symptoms. Research is also underway into the use of fish oil supplements to treat problems of attention-deficit disorder or hyperactivity as it is hoped that increased levels of omega-3 fatty acids may help to calm aggression, and improve attention and concentration. However, there are, of course, many other contributing factors.

Arthritis

There are two common types of arthritis: osteoarthritis which develops in older age as the joints – particularly knees and hips – become less well lubricated and rub together, causing damage. Knee and hip replacements are common. Rheumatoid arthritis is a type of inflammation of the membranes in the joints, resulting in swelling and pain, and sufferers can be younger.

Adjusting the diet is a recognized way of helping to ease the symptoms of the rheumatoid form of arthritis. The fish oils can also help in alleviating the painful symptoms associated with arthritis. Cod liver oil has been used in the treatment of arthritis since the middle of the last century, so introducing the idea of a healthy diet rich in fish and low in saturated fats is not new.

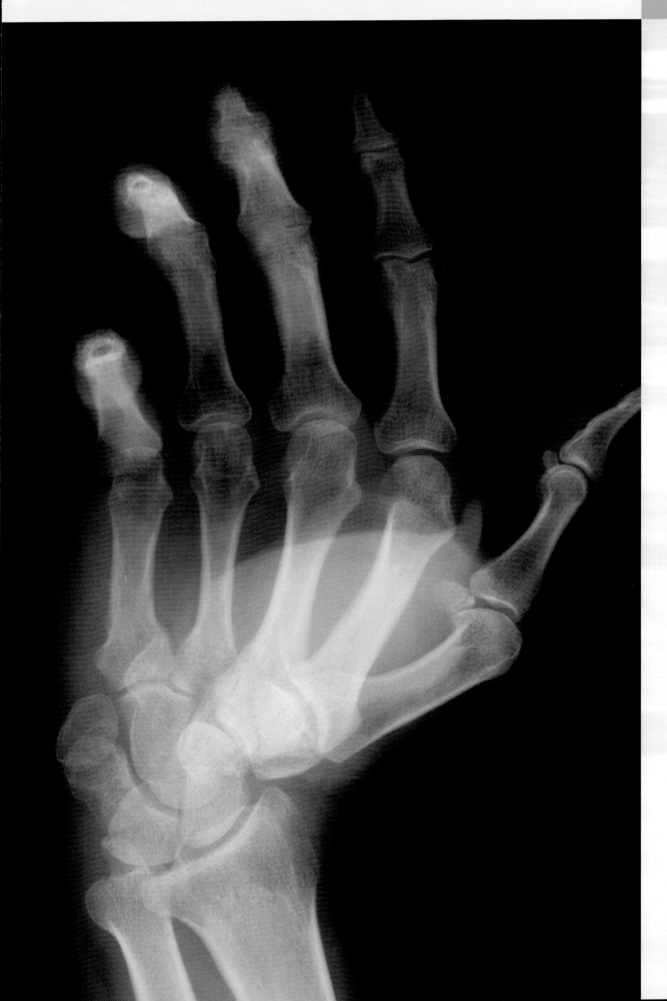

ESSENTIAL EATING:
FOOD FOR WELLBEING

Good eating is personal and there are no hard and fast rules that can be applied as requirements vary within flexible guidelines according to lifestyle, metabolism and taste. Maintaining a healthy weight is one fundamental, and sometimes difficult, requirement that depends on balancing diet with any one individual capacity for burning calories. As well as eating appropriate quantities, it is important to include the right mix and proportion of foods on a regular basis.

There are no such things as unhealthy foods, but some items can be eaten in unhealthy quantities. Avoiding complete categories of food for no good reason can also result in deficiencies because valuable nutrients are excluded. There is no great secret to good eating – it is all about variety and balance, which means establishing an enjoyable, long-term diet. Eating lots of different types of food provides a good range of nutrients; at the same time, individual foods are less likely to be eaten in unhealthily large quantities.

Balancing a diet means eating different types of food in the proportions the body needs them. The general recommendation is to include plenty of plant foods and ample supplies of starch, a good fibre content, modest amounts of low-fat protein, oily fish and a little fat. The other basic requirement is to eat more-or-less the right amount for the energy expended to avoid becoming unhealthily overweight.

Getting it Right

Eating fish regularly is valuable to health, especially the oily fish, which should be included twice a week, along with white fish as an excellent low-fat protein food. Including plenty of fish in the diet is only part of the story and the following puts the protein portion into perspective alongside a good mixture of other foods.

Starchy carbohydrates – foods like bread, potatoes, pasta, rice and other grains – are the best source of energy for the body. They are satisfying and the right type of food to fill up on.

Fruit and vegetables are vital for vitamins and minerals as well as other benefits and they should be eaten in generous quantities. Health experts recommend that five portions of fruit and vegetables should be eaten daily. Plant foods in particular play a valuable protective role. The importance of vitamins, minerals and fibre is well established; the extent of the contribution from other components in plant foods is only just being discovered.

Proteins are essential for growth and repair of the body, but they are not needed in as large a proportion as vegetables and starches. Animal sources of protein – including fish, poultry and meat – should be balanced by vegetable proteins, such as beans and pulses.

Fats are important in the diet, but only in modest proportions, so foods that are high in fat should not be eaten regularly in large quantities. Animal fats, in particular, should be limited.

A Guide to Nutrients

The functions of separate nutrients may be different but they work closely together to keep the body machine running smoothly.

Carbohydrates These are starches (complex carbohydrates) and sugars (simple carbohydrates). They are the satisfying foods and the energy providers. Starchy foods should form the base for a healthy diet. Energy is released slowly from complex carbohydrates, so not only do they feel filling when first eaten but they also provide a steady source of energy for some time.

It is important to eat starches that are unrefined and high in fibre as well as the more refined types. For example, some wholemeal bread should be included as well as white bread. Breakfast cereals and whole grains are also valuable.

Fibre This is carbohydrate that the body cannot digest and break down completely, so it is passed out of the body. It absorbs liquid to provide bulk and moisture for the waste products of digestion, allowing them to be excreted easily and preventing constipation. There are different types of fibre, some from fruit and vegetables and other from starchy carbohydrates. A good mixture of different types, including soluble fibre from oats and the pectin content of fruit, is helpful for moderating cholesterol levels.

Sugars these occur naturally in some vegetables and many fruits, and these naturally sweet foods can make good sweeteners instead of using pure sugar. There is nothing wrong with sugar but it can be eaten to excess as it provides 'empty' calories. Eating lots of sugary snacks and sweet foods can result in a weight problem. High-sugar snacks and sweet, acidic drinks cause dental caries, particularly in children and young people. Children should be encouraged to avoid developing a 'sweet tooth' by giving them diluted juices that are low in sugar, and by including raw fruit and vegetables as healthy snacks. There is nothing wrong with sweets as an occasional treat, but not as a regular part of the diet.

Protein

Fish, poultry and meat are the main animal protein foods; dairy produce, such as eggs, cheese and milk, is also a source. Proteins are made up of amino acids, eight of which are essential and they are all provided in animal protein. Plant sources of protein do not include all the essential amino acids in any one food, with the exception of soya beans, which are a source of high-quality protein. Other beans and pulses, rice and grains provide protein. When a good mix of vegetable foods is eaten, the body obtains all the amino acids it needs.

Fat

Fatty acids are essential in the diet. Fats are known as saturated or unsaturated: the unsaturated fats may be polyunsaturated or mono-unsaturated. Animal fats tend to have a higher content of saturated fat than vegetable fats. The amount of the fat in the diet should be limited to a small amount daily and the majority of the fat we eat should be unsaturated. High-fat foods, such as butter, cheese, cream, fatty meats, oils and oil-based spreads and dressings, should be used in modest amounts. Oily fish should be eaten regularly – ideally twice a week – to provide the valuable omega-3 fatty acids (see page 11).

Vitamins

Vitamins are found in a wide variety of foods and they fulfill many general or specific functions. These are the catalysts that spark off essential bodily processes, or ensure that they work successfully. They also help to protect the body against infection, disease and damage, and maintain general good health. Vitamins are grouped into water-soluble types – vitamins C and B group, and fat-soluble types – vitamins A, D, E and K.

Water-Soluble Vitamins

The body does not store water-soluble vitamins for any length of time and excess intakes are excreted, so the diet must include regular supplies. These vitamins also seep out of food into cooking liquids. They are sensitive to heat and light, and the levels contained in food diminish with staleness.

Although the fat-soluble vitamins are stored in the body, they are still required regularly but they can be eaten to excess. These vitamins are not as easily lost during food preparation and boiling, but they are lost with fat during roasting, frying and grilling (broiling).

Vitamin C is found in fruit and vegetables. It is essential for healthy tissue and known as the vitamin that is vital for good skin. It is necessary for the process of absorbing and utilizing other nutrients, such as iron. Vitamin C is also an antioxidant, helping to protect the body and repair damage caused by free radicals.

The **B-group** vitamins are important for metabolism, the breaking down, absorbing and using of food. They also fulfil other vital tasks, including maintaining a healthy nervous system and generating red blood cells.

Vitamin B1 or thiamin is found in meat and offal, wholegrains, nuts, beans and pulses. It is important for the nervous system and in ensuring that the body can release and use energy from food.

Vitamin B2 or riboflavin is found in meat, offal, eggs, milk and its products, fish, and fortified cereals and flours. Riboflavin helps the body to release and use energy from food.

Riboflavin is light sensitive – so the content diminishes in milk which is left to stand in the sun.

Niacin or nicotinic acid is found in poultry, meat, fish, nuts and vegetables. It is essential for cell function and the passing of messages through the nervous system. It is also important for the release and use of energy.

Vitamin B6 or pyridoxine is found in many foods, including fish, poultry, meat, vegetables, cereals, nuts and yeast extract. It is important for the formation of red blood cells, for a healthy immune system and for breaking down protein.

Vitamin B12 or cobalamin is found in animal foods, including fish, poultry, meat, eggs and dairy produce. It is also found in fortified breakfast cereals. This vitamin is essential for producing DNA and so it is vital for all cell generation, including the formation of red blood cells. Since it is widely available in foods, deficiency is rare; however, those following a vegan diet, excluding all animal products, are vulnerable.

Folate or folic acid is found in green vegetables, liver, wheatgerm and fortified cereals. It is essential for the production of red blood cells and all DNA. It is particularly important before conception and during pregnancy for the development of the baby.

Pantothenic acid is found in most foods, including meat and offal, vegetables, dried fruit and nuts. It is assists in the release of energy and the manufacture of red blood cells, cholesterol and fat.

Fat-Soluble Vitamins

Vitamin A or retinol is found in animal foods, such as oily fish, liver, milk and its products, and eggs. Beta-carotene is converted into vitamin A in the body: it is found in highly coloured fruit and vegetables, including carrots, red and orange (bell) peppers, mangoes, apricots and green leafy vegetables. Vitamin A is important for healthy eyes and good night vision, as well as cell construction, the mucous membranes in the eyes, and for the respiratory and digestive tracts. Vitamin A promotes healthy skin and is used for general cell building.

Vitamin D is found in liver, oily fish, eggs and fortified margarines. It is also synthesized in the body when it is exposed to sunlight. Deficiency is rare, except in those who are confined to the indoors, such as the elderly. Vitamin D is important for calcium and phosphorus absorption, therefore for healthy bones and teeth.

Vitamin E is found in vegetable fats and oils, including nuts and seeds, oils and avocado. Vitamin E is an important antioxidant, protecting the body for damage caused by free radicals.

Vitamin K is found in green leafy vegetables. It is important for the normal clotting of the blood.

Minerals

Minerals assist with specific and general functions throughout the body. Some minerals are required in small amounts but they are still important and the body must have an adequate supply.

Calcium is found in milk and milk products, sardines and other fish where the bones are eaten (such as canned salmon), shellfish, dark leafy green vegetables and sesame seeds. The oxalic acid in spinach and phytic acid in the outer layers of whole grains both inhibit the absorption of calcium. Vitamin D is also essential for calcium absorption. Calcium is important for healthy bones and teeth.

Copper is found in a wide range of foods and deficiency is rare. Liver, shellfish, nuts and mushrooms all provide copper. It is important for iron absorption, the manufacture of red blood cells and connective tissue, and to help protect the body against damage from free radicals.

Fluorine is found in fish but the main dietary source, to varying degrees, is water, depending on the soil and local policies on the fluoridation of tap water. It is important for the enamel coating on teeth and for healthy bones but an excess can be damaging, causing the overformation or hardening of bones.

Iodine is found in seafood, including seaweed, vegetables and fruit. The level of iodine in food depends on the soil, with more in coastal areas. Iodine is essential, in small amounts, for a healthy thyroid gland and the levels of hormones it produces to control energy production, as well as for growth and development. Iodine deficiency leads to an under-active thyroid gland, a common symptom of which is a general lack of energy.

Iron is found in meat and offal, egg yolks and green leafy vegetables. Iron from vegetables, such as spinach and watercress, is not as easily absorbed as that from animal sources. Vitamin C aids iron absorption, so it is helpful to combine foods rich in vitamin C with those rich in iron. The body limits the amount of iron that it will absorb and store, so the diet must include a regular supply. Iron is important for haemoglobin or red blood cell production and for the proper functioning of enzymes.

Magnesium is found in dairy produce, grains, pulses, green vegetables and nuts, as well as many other foods. Deficiency is rare in a good mixed diet. It is important for enzyme activity and the function of the nervous system and muscles.

Manganese is found in plant foods in levels that depend on the amount in the soil. It is obtained from whole grains, pulses and nuts. Its roles include enzyme activity, proper thyroid function, insulin production, muscle and nerve function. Deficiency is rare in a healthy mixed diet.

Molybdenum is widely distributed in plant foods and liver, and deficiency is rare. Its is important for proper enzyme function.

Phosphorus is found in animal foods, plants and whole grains, and deficiency is rare. It is vital for healthy bones and teeth, and for energy production. It is also found in, and is important to the function of, body proteins. It is so widely available that deficiency is rare but it can be eaten to excess. The phosphorus and calcium in the diet should be balanced, as too much phosphorus can make the body reduce its calcium absorption, resulting in calcium deficiency. Phosphorus and calcium are found in the same natural foods; however, phosphorus is found in processed foods in the form of phosphates (compounds of phosphorus) and diets with a high content of processed foods, rich in phosphates but low in calcium, can lead to an imbalance.

Potassium is found in most foods, especially meat, whole grains, vegetables, celery, citrus fruit and bananas. With sodium, potassium is important for bodily fluid balance and efficient nerve and muscle activity.

Selenium is widely available in fish, meat, offal, dairy produce, citrus fruit, grains and avocados. Levels in plant sources relate to those in the soil. Selenium plays roles in hormone activity, growth and development. It is important for healthy eyes and hair, and as an antioxidant, helping to protect against damage from free radicals.

Sodium is found in sodium chloride or salt. It is essential, with potassium, for balancing fluid levels in the body, and for nerve and muscle function. Salt is so widely used that diets can have too high a sodium content, especially when lots of processed and prepared products (generally containing lots of salt) are eaten regularly. A diet with a very high salt content contributes to the problem of high blood pressure. Sodium is lost in sweat, so levels have to be replenished.

Sulphur is a compound found in proteins, so it is available from animal foods, fish and pulses. It is important in body proteins, including skin, hair, nails and connective tissue, and is also vital to many hormone functions in the body.

Zinc is found in fish and shellfish, as well as all animal foods and whole grains. Zinc in animal foods is more readily absorbed than that in vegetable sources. It is important for enzyme activity and for the activity of the immune system, for night vision, taste and digestion, and energy production.

Phytochemicals

In addition to well-documented nutrients, many thousand plant substances contribute to health. Plant chemicals or phytochemicals are thought to protect the body against disease and its causes, particularly against free radicals which latch on to cells in the body or oxidize them.

Plant chemicals include the carotenoids. Carotenes or carotenoids are well known, particularly beta-carotene, the substance that gives carrots and other vegetables and fruit their strong colour. Lycopene is the carotenoid in tomatoes. Allicin is a substance found in plants of the onion family. A vast group of substances, known as glucosolinates, are found in the crucifera family of vegetables, which includes mustard greens, cabbage, curly kale, Brussels sprouts, broccoli, cauliflower, swede (rutabaga) and radishes. Flavonoids or bio-flavonoids include thousands of different substances that are often associated with vegetables with a slightly sweet flavour because they contain glucose compounds. Phytoestrogens are plant chemicals found in a variety of plant foods. They are similar to oestrogen, the femal sex hormone, and their activity is similar to that of the hormone.

HERE'S SEAFOOD:
AN AMAZING CHOICE

Seafood is the term for all types of fish, shellfish and edible plants that are harvested from the sea and used for food. This includes an incredible array of species from all over the world. Seafood can be cooked by as many methods and in as many different dishes as there are eating cultures.

For culinary purposes, fish is divided into either white or oily types. Fish from tropical waters and types that are not commonly available in Western displays are usually referred to as exotic fish. Another useful division is between flat and round fish, according to body shape.

White Fish

White fish is low in fat, with the oil concentrated in the liver. The flesh is pale with a comparatively delicate flavour, which varies according to the type of fish. White fish can be further divided into round or flat. The following is a brief summary of the main types of white fish – all are low in fat and can be cooked by almost any method. American names or alternatives are given in brackets where appropriate, and are included in the ingredients list of each recipe.

Bream (Snapper)

There are many varieties, including red, black and gilt head sea bream. The breams yield white fillets, varying in eating quality according to the particular fish.

Cod

A large white fish of the round type with firm, very white flesh in large flakes and a delicate flavour. Available in fillets or steaks.

Coley (Pollock; Cod)

A member of the same family as cod, this has a coarser texture and stronger flavour. The large flakes are slightly grey in colour. Available in fillets.

Conger Eel

A round fish with firm, lightly flavoured flesh that is cut into steaks. Suitable for stewing and braising or roasting.

Dab (Flounder; Sole)

A small flat fish which provides good-quality white flesh. Cooked whole.

Dory (Oreo John Dory)

Also known as the John Dory, this extremely ugly specimen yields white fillets of good quality.

Flounder (Sole)

Flat fish related to plaice but not considered to be as good quality.

Gurnard (Sea Robin)

There are various types of this ugly fish, including red and grey gurnards. They are sold whole or in fillets and have firm, white flesh.

Haddock (Blue cod; Hoki)

A member of the cod family, the flesh of this smaller fish is slightly finer and the flakes are not quite as large and firm as those of cod. The flavour is good and sweet. Available in steaks.

Hake (Silver Hake)

A firm white fish with large moist flakes and a delicate, slightly sweet flavour. Hake is a cartilaginous fish with large bones but few of them. Prepared in steaks or fillets.

Halibut

A large flat, white fish, the halibut has firm flesh and a fine flavour. Sold in fillets or steaks.

Hoki

A species popular in New Zealand and Australia, this firm white fish has a delicate flavour similar to cod or haddock. Sold in fillets.

Huss (Shark)

A white round fish of the shark family, with a light flavour and firm cartilaginous texture. Also called Rock Salmon or Dogfish.Sold in fillets or steaks, suitable for stewing or frying.

Lemon Sole (English Sole; Flounder)

A flat fish with fine-textured flesh and a delicate flavour. In spite of its name this is not a true sole but it is still a high-quality fish. Sold whole or in fillets.

Monkfish (Anglerfish)

A large fish with a huge, ugly head, it is the fillets off the tail that are sold skinned and ready for cooking. The flesh is firm, white and moist with an excellent flavour. It is suitable for all cooking methods.

Mullet (Striped Bass0

Red mullet is a small, round fish with red skin and delicate white flesh that has a good flavour. Cooked whole or in fillets. Grey mullet is larger, with firm white flesh and a good flavour, but not of the fine quality of red mullet.

Plaice (Flounder; Sole)

Flat white fish with fine-textured flesh and a distinctive but delicate flavour. Sold whole or in fillets.

Sea Bass

Round white fish with an excellent flavour and fine texture. Sold whole or in fillets.

Shark

Various members of the shark family of fish are used in cooking. These fish have cartilaginous skeletons rather than the usual network of fine bones found in fish. The firm, coarse-textured flesh is sold in steaks.

Skate

A cartilaginous fish with fins developed into large wings that are the edible portion. Very fresh skate smells of ammonia, an odour that subsides and disappears when the wings are rinsed several times in cold water or blanched in a little boiling water before cooking.

Sole (English Sole; Gray Sole)

There are several types of this flat fish, with Dover sole being the most prized for its fine texture and excellent flavour. Sold whole or in fillets.

Swordfish

A large fish with firm, meaty and dry white flesh. Sold in steaks.

Turbot (Flounder; Gray Sole)

A very large flat fish with firm white flesh that is prized for its excellent flavour.

Whiting

A round white fish with firm, fairly fine flesh and a light, almost bland, flavour. Sold whole or in fillets.

Oily Fish

These are more distinct in flavour that the white fish and their flesh is packed full of goodness. The smaller fish may be cooked whole or in fillets. Their oil content makes these fish ideal for barbecuing and grilling (broiling). Their fat content also means that these fish do not keep as well as white fish.

Anchovy

A small oily fish with a full flavour. Away from the Mediterranean countries where they are fished and eaten as a fresh-fish delicacy or sold preserved in salt straight from the barrel, the common international form is canned or bottled in oil.

Herring

A small fish with a good flavour. The herring has lots of very fine bones which are off-putting to many. Sold whole or in fillets. Smoked herring are known as kippers.

Mackerel

A fish with a full flavour and fine, delicious flesh, the mackerel is best eaten when young and small. Sold whole or in fillets, mackerel quickly deteriorates in quality and has to be sold and cooked when fresh.

Salmon

A large migratory fish that moves from salt to fresh water. Now farmed to a vast extent by methods that are currently being exposed as extremely undesirable in many cases. The firm, full-flavoured flesh of wild salmon is delicious and superior to that of farmed salmon. Sold whole, in steaks or fillets.

Sardine

Young fish of the herring family, known as pilchard when fully grown, with a full, delicious flavour. These small fish are popular for barbecues and grills.

Tuna

Large fish including several related species all with firm, meaty flesh. Tuna ranges in colour from a dusky pink to dark brown-red. The paler flesh has the finer flavour and texture. Sold in steaks, this is suitable for all cooking methods.

Whitebait (Smelt)

Tiny fish, the fry of different species, usually herring and sprat. These are cooked whole by coating in flour and deep-frying – after which they are crisp and delicious.

Exotic Fish

The term exotic fish is applied to species that are fished in tropical waters and to those that are not regularly available in plentiful supply. These include fish such as snappers, a term covering several types of fish all with large jaws and sharp teeth; the parrot fish, named for having a beak-shaped jaw and bright-coloured skin; and emperors, the name applied to various colourful fish.

Shellfish

Shellfish are a low-fat source of protein and B vitamins, especially B12. They also provide selenium, a mineral required for healthy thyroid function, and which also protects against damage from free radicals.

The shellfish may be divided into crustaceans and molluscs. The crustaceans are covered by a hinged amour of shell. The molluscs can be further divided into bivalves, such as scallops and mussels, with two hinged shells, and univalves, such as winkles.

The cholesterol found in shellfish, particularly high in prawns and shrimps, does not seem to be absorbed readily by the human body. Studies indicate the a shellfish-rich diet does not result in an increase in blood cholesterol.

Crustaceans

Crab

There are hundreds of species of crab. The common crab with a brown or red shell has large front claws that contain a good quantity of excellent white meat. The brown meat is extracted from the inside of the body parts and shell. Crab is a good source of zinc as well as B vitamins and potassium.

Lobster

Lobster is almost black in colour when alive, only turning bright red during the cooking process. The meat from lobster is firm, white and succulent, with a delicate sweet flavour. This is one of the most prized shellfish. In addition to providing the same nutrients as other seafood, lobster is a good source of selenium.

Prawns and Shrimps

There are many types of prawns and shrimps, ranging from the tiny brown shrimps (that remain brown in colour when cooked) to jumbo, king or Mediterranean prawns. There are little pink shrimps as well as the brown-shelled variety, but they do not have the same fabulous flavour. Cold-water prawns are smaller and slightly softer in texture than warm-water species, which range from firm, slightly larger examples through different sizes of tiger prawns – so-called because of their stripes. (Americans tend to use the word 'shrimp' to cover prawns as well as shrimps.)

The smaller cold-water prawns are sold cooked and shelled, with medium to large examples available cooked and in their shells. The larger warm-water prawns are available raw or cooked, in their shells or peeled.

Molluscs

Clams

There are many varieties of clam, ranging from tiny examples similar to cockles to giant specimens. While the small types are tender and require brief cooking, the larger varieties become tender only after gentle stewing. Clams are a good source of iron.

Cockles

There are several types of these small bivalves, which are a good source of iron. They are usually eaten cooked, but some types are also savoured raw.

Mussels (Blue Mussels)

There are various types of these succulent, flavoursome bivalves. The green-lipped New Zealand mussels are considerable larger than the common European types. Mussels provide iron and iodine, and vitamin E as well as folate and the B group vitamins found in other shellfish.

Oysters

There are many types of oyster, among which the European and Pacific are key types. The European oyster is more rounded in shape and smaller than the elongated Pacific oyster. Oysters are rich in zinc and copper; they also provide iron, potassium, selenium and iodine. Oysters have a delicate flavour which is enjoyed raw or lightly cooked.

Scallops (Sea/Bay Scallops)

These delicate shellfish have a light flavour and tender texture. They consist of a nugget of firm white meat with a bright red curve of roe or coral attached. Queen (Bay) scallops, or queens, are small and round, and do not contain any coral.

Smoked Fish

Smoked fish provides the same goodness as unsmoked and it makes a delicious contribution to good eating. The vitamin and omega-3 benefits are not lost by smoking. Smoked white fish, such as haddock and cod, are excellent poached or steamed and served with poached eggs or used in simple dishes, such as fish pie and kedgeree (turmeric-spiced rice with smoked haddock and boiled eggs).

Smoked mackerel is versatile and delicious for hot and cold dishes – flaked and tossed with pasta or rice; in chunks and tossed with new potatoes for an irresistible salad; with salad leaves, avocado and tomato – the options are endless. Kippers and bloaters are smoked forms of herring – excellent poached or grilled (broiled) and served plain or flaked and used in a variety of dishes.

Smoked salmon is also versatile and economical enough to be used in small quantities in slightly special everyday dishes. Hot smoked salmon is similar to smoked mackerel in that it is cooked, rather than moist and raw, and cut thick. Smoked halibut is similar to smoked salmon in texture, but pale in colour, delicate in flavour and more expensive. It makes a luxurious alternative to the now commonplace smoked salmon, particularly served with a watercress salad, wholemeal or rye bread and a little low-fat crème fraîche as an appetizer or light lunch.

It has to be acknowledged that there is some evidence to suggest that we should not consume smoked foods too frequently because of a danger that the smoking process may contribute cancer-encouraging carcinogens. However, in this context, smoking includes chargrilled (charbroiled) and highly flavoured products and the frequent use of extremely hot grilling (broiling) or barbecuing to singe the surface of food.

Fish Roe

Roe is the name for fish eggs. Soft roe is the term for the male testis or milt, while hard roe is the term for the eggs of the female. Available fresh or canned, roes provide protein (more in the hard roe) and fat (more in the soft roe), vitamins A, D and E. Smoked cod's roe is the ingredient used to make taramasalata – the Greek pâté or dip of puréed roe with olive oil, garlic and lemon. Canned roes, soft or hard, are traditionally served on toast as a snack but they are also good with garlic, herbs, olive oil and lemon for a quick dip or pâté.

Canned fish is a brilliant convenience food for instant cold dishes, sandwich fillings and toast toppings. Canned sardines and anchovies provide omega-3 fatty acids but tuna is not a rich source because the fat is removed before canning. However, canned tuna is still a versatile storecupboard ingredient that makes a valuable and tasty contribution to well-balanced eating.

Convenient Fish

Frozen fish is an excellent alternative to fresh. It retains all the food value and benefits of fresh fish, and the best is good quality. Products with fat-rich coatings are not the same as straightforward fresh fish. Fish fingers are a good example: they are popular with children but just look at how greasy the coating becomes when cooked – even during grilling (broiling) – for evidence of excess fat. They are fine once in a while but their flavour is strongly biased towards the coating rather than the fish.

Cephalopods

This group of strange-looking seafood includes the familiar squid as well as the octopus and cuttlefish. These creatures are characterized by having their body parts sprouting from their heads and by their ink sacs. Squid is the most readily available of the three, often sold prepared with the head removed, leaving an elongated, empty white sac of thin tender flesh. The tentacles of the squid can be used in cooking. The cleaned-out head and tentacles of octopus are used in cooking. As well as providing low-fat protein, these include the B vitamins and selenium; squid also provides iodine.

Sea Plants

Various types of seaweed are put to culinary use, including dulse, eaten in Ireland, Scotland, France and Iceland as well as North America. Kelp is widely used in Japanese cooking, under the name of kombu, especially for making light stock, known as dashi. Nori is another popular Japanese seaweed, known particularly as the shiny, toasted thin sheets that are used for making sushi (moulded or shaped rice). Laver is the Welsh name for the same seaweed, this time cooked and puréed for making oat-coated patties. Seaweeds are rich in minerals, particularly iodine.

Samphire is a plant found growing along the coastline. Its long, fine, cylindrical and slightly knobbly stems are crunchy with a salty flavour. The minimum of cooking ensures that samphire retains its pleasing texture – either blanch it briefly or stir-fry it quickly in a little olive oil or unsalted (sweet) butter. Do not add salt during cooking, but serve with plenty of black pepper and lemon juice.

SIMPLE SEAFOOD:
COOKING MADE EASY

The terrific truth is that nothing could be easier than making a superbly simple seafood meal. Fish and seafood are readily available as pure and natural ingredients, requiring little or no preparation and speedy cooking. Here is the versatile, healthy and delicious main food choice for good balanced eating. If you are unused to cooking from scratch, all you need is a little confidence when it comes to making wonderful meals – just try some of these basic methods before creating more complicated recipes and you will soon appreciate the benefits of fish. Once you are into the habit of eating fish as part of a well-balanced diet, the feel-good factor will kick in and you will be inspired to sample all the recipes the following chapters have to offer.

Familiarity with Fishmongers

There is no need to fret about preparation as all supermarkets sell seafood ready for cooking. Check out the freezers as well as the chiller cabinets and fresh fish counter because good-quality frozen fish is worth eating and it is a valuable 'storecupboard' ingredient for keeping in the freezer. On factory ships, fish is frozen promptly after being caught, providing fillets and steaks that are (often) free from skin and bones, and ideal for cooking from frozen.

Supermarket fresh fish counters and traditional fishmongers are geared up to providing an individual service, so do not be shy about asking for ingredients to be prepared. Cleaning (or gutting), filleting, trimming, boning and skinning are all part of the service you can expect, and it will be carried out in the flash of a sharp blade to a standard far higher than the amateur, occasional fish-cook can achieve.

Selecting Fish and Seafood

When buying from a wet fish counter, look over the display for quality and care. The fish and seafood should be neatly displayed on well-frozen ice, every item clearly laid out with care. Displays piled with excess quantities of fish that look as though they have been thrown down are usually indicative of a lack of understanding and care for the food.

The area should smell clean and fresh – if there is the slightest hint of a bad smell, walk away. (If you are dealing with a large supermarket, make sure the store manager is aware that you are unhappy with the standard and would like to see an improvement.) The fish should be undamaged and neat, and look firm, moist and fresh. Skin and eyes should be moist, shiny and bright. Shellfish should have undamaged shells, be moist and a good colour. Lobster and crab should feel heavy for their size and should not contain water (shake them to check if they make swooshing noises); when live, they should be just that – lively rather than lethargic. Live bivalves (mussels, oysters) should have firmly shut shells.

Packaged fresh fish from chiller cabinets should display the same qualities. All packages should be clean, undamaged and marked with a date by which they should be sold and the contents used. Frozen fish should be well packaged and marked with a date by which it should be eaten. The contents should look good – avoid fish fillets that look dried and white on the surface as this indicates freezer burn, a result of poor packaging. Packs of prawns or seafood full of ice should also be avoided. All chiller cabinets and freezers should be clean, neatly packed and not overfilled.

Healthy Cooking Methods Made Easy

The methods to use for cooking everyday meals are those that do not require a large quantity of additional fat. The following is a general summary of different cooking methods and the ways in which they can be used for healthy seafood meals. With a few tough examples – such as large squid and octopus – fish and seafood requires comparatively brief cooking. Overcooking is to be avoided at all costs – leave delicate fish cooking for too long and the flesh will quickly dry out, harden or break up, and lose much of its flavour.

Storing Seafood

- Chill seafood as soon as possible after purchase and make sure frozen items are transferred to your freezer promptly before they have time to thaw.

- Leave chilled packages unopened and place in the fridge. Use by the date recommended on the packet.

- Unwrap loose-packed seafood and place it on a dish or deep plate, then cover with cling film (saran wrap) and chill. Use on the same day or day after purchase.

Boiling

The dated idea of boiling being a suitable method for delicate white fish is far short of the truth – the flesh is far too delicate for such a harsh method. However, boiling is a traditional means of killing live shellfish but this requires a huge cooking pot and, in my opinion, a good deal of courage. Plunging live lobster or crab into a huge pot of rapidly boiling water and firmly slapping on the lid is one method of dealing with the shellfish.

(The alternative of stabbing behind the head is barely easier, while freezing seems more humane and satisfactory, especially given that it is a method less likely to go pitifully wrong with the result of extending the suffering of the creature involved.)

Poaching

This is an excellent method for delicate fish and seafood. The poaching liquid may be water, court bouillon, stock, wine or milk. Ingredients to be served hot or cold, plain or sauced, with or without the cooking liquor, can be cooked by this method. A fish kettle or large, deep, flameproof roasting tin should be used for poaching large fish (use foil to cover a roasting tin instead of a lid). A turbot kettle is a large, diamond-shaped cooking pot designed to hold the large flat fish. A deep lidded skillet or frying pan (skillet) is suitable for steaks, fillets and smaller whole fish.

Prepare the poaching liquid first. Add a bay leaf, a few sprigs of parsley and a strip of pared lemon rind with some black peppercorns and a sprinkling of salt. Heat the liquid gently until boiling, then cover and simmer gently for 5-10 minutes. Remove from the heat and leave to cool so that the liquid is infused with the flavouring ingredients.

Add the fish to the liquid and heat gently until barely simmering, then cover and cook very gently, never allowing the liquid to simmer too rapidly. Whole fish should be about half to two-thirds immersed in the liquid. Steaks and fillets should be just covered with liquid. When cooking large whole fish to be served cold, such as salmon, allow about 4–5 minutes per 450 g/1 lb, in liquid that is barely bubbling. Then remove the pan from the heat and leave the fish to cool in the liquid – this ensures that the flesh remains moist.

Cooking Times

Fillets take 5–10 minutes for small portions or up to 15 minutes for large pieces. Small whole fish take about 15 minutes.

Healthy Serving

- Use cooking liquors based on stock or wine to make a light sauce by boiling them until reduced to a small quantity once the fish has been removed. Strain the liquor and taste it for seasoning before serving. The basic liquor can be enriched with a little low-fat Greek-style yogurt or fromage frais (add this off the heat or it will curdle).

- Dress the poached fish or seafood with warmed, flavoured oil. Heat a little olive oil with a little grated lemon or lime zest or chopped fresh herbs. For a stronger dressing, heat a halved garlic clove in the oil, stirring it to extract some flavour but discarding it before pouring the oil over the fish.

- Make a light salad dressing of lemon juice with olive oil (1 tablespoon lemon juice to 3 tablespoons olive oil), a little sugar, salt and pepper, and 1 teaspoon mild wholegrain mustard in a small saucepan. Bring to the boil, whisking, and remove from the heat. Allow to cool until warm, then whisk in some chopped fresh dill (dill weed). Trickle a little of this over the poached fish.

Steaming

Steaming is an excellent method for bringing out the natural flavour of the fish and ingredients cooked with it. Adding a little butter or olive oil enriches the dish but it is not necessary. Methods range from placing the ingredients in a perforated steamer, strewing them with aromatic herbs and cooking over boiling water, to enclosing the fish in foil or greaseproof (waxed) paper packages with flavouring ingredients. Alternatively the fish may be arranged on a greased plate and covered tightly with foil, then placed like a lid over a saucepan of simmering water.

To cook fish in a package, cut a piece of foil large enough to hold the fish and brush the foil with a little olive oil. Arrange the fish – fillets, steaks or small whole fish – on the middle of the foil. Top with bay leaves, a few sprigs of parsley or tarragon and some chives, and add a slice of lemon to each portion. Season lightly, then wrap the foil tightly around the fish. Place in a steamer over a pan of boiling water.

Cooking Times

Fine-cut to medium-cut fillets take 5–10 minutes. Large, thick fillets, steaks and small whole fish require 15–20 minutes.

Healthy Serving

- Make a fresh salsa of 6 finely chopped ripe tomatoes, 1 tablespoon tomato purée, salt and pepper, 1 teaspoon sugar, the grated zest and juice of ½ lemon and 2 tablespoons olive oil. Add plenty of chopped fresh parsley and a finely chopped garlic clove, if liked. Cover and leave to marinate for a few hours, if possible, before serving. Great with poached, steamed, grilled or baked fish and far healthier than a rich sauce.

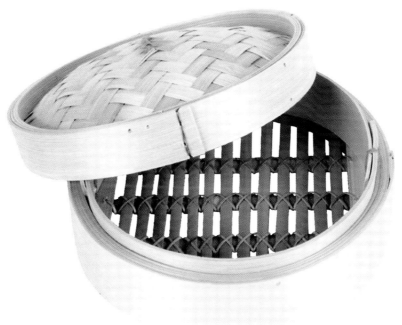

Braising and Casseroling

Many types of fish are ideal for braising or casseroling – stewing, even – in a good sauce. The trick is to match the cooking time for the sauce with the type of fish. For example, firm, meaty swordfish or tuna require longer cooking than lighter but chunky cod. Whereas with poultry and meat you can allow the sauce to cook at the same time as the main ingredient, with fish and seafood it is generally a good idea to prepare and simmer the cooking medium – the sauce – until it is quite mellow before adding the fish. Onions, carrots, celery, fennel, garlic and similar ingredients should be sautéed or sweated in a covered pan until tender before the liquid is added. Canned tomatoes and a little white wine, cider or stock are all suitable. Bring the sauce to the boil, then cover the pan and simmer gently for at least 15 minutes, or longer, depending on how quickly the chosen fish will cook.

Then add the fish, shuffling the pieces into the sauce. Alternatively, pour the sauce over the fish in an ovenproof casserole. It is a good idea to roll or fold fine fillets as this makes their shape more even, protecting the thin ends by rolling them up in the thick ends. Cover and finish cooking by simmering very gently on the hob or in the oven at about 160–180°C/325–350°F/Gas 3–4 (use the higher cooking temperature for thicker, meatier fish).

Cooking Times

Small cuts will take 15–20 minutes; medium portions about 30 minutes; larger or thick pieces 40–45 minutes. The precise cooking time will vary according to the other ingredients in the casserole.

Healthy Serving

• Toss boiled rice with chopped fresh parsley and/or grated lemon zest to complement fish casseroles.

• Fork plenty of finely snipped chives and chopped fresh tarragon into couscous to make a full-flavoured base for hearty fish and seafood casseroles.

• Stir-fry diced or sliced courgettes (zucchini) and some cut green beans in a little olive oil and then toss them with cooked pasta. Add plenty of chopped watercress to make a healthy accompaniment.

Baking

As a general rule, bake fish in a covered dish or wrapped in foil to retain moisture. Grease the dish with a little butter or olive oil. The dish should be large enough to hold all the portions or fish without having to overlap them too much. Overlapping the fish can create very thick areas that are shielded from the heat, therefore requiring longer cooking than the fish in other areas.

Chopped and/or diced vegetables, such as onion, carrot, fennel and/or celery, can be cooked in a little olive oil first until softened and laid in the bottom of the dish before adding the fish. Bay leaves, sprigs of fresh herbs and pared strips of lemon, lime or orange rind are all flavouring ingredients that can be laid in the bottom of the dish.

Season the fish to taste and top with a little butter or oil, or sprinkle with lemon juice before covering. Turn steaks or whole fish halfway through cooking. Bake at 180°C/ 350° F/Gas 4.

Alternatively, top fish steaks or fillets with a breadcrumb stuffing or mixture of crumbs and chopped herbs. Sprinkle with a little grated cheese or trickle with a little olive oil to moisten and brown the topping. Bake uncovered.

Cooking Times

Allow 20–30 minutes for fish rolls, steaks and fillets. Small whole fish require about 30 minutes and slightly larger whole fish take 35–40 minutes.

Healthy Serving

• Creamy mashed potatoes, moistened with a little olive oil instead of too much butter, and a crisp salad of mixed leaves, finely cut green or red (bell) peppers, and cherry tomatoes are excellent accompaniments for baked fish.

• Bake potato wedges to go with plainly baked fish fillets. Cut thick wedges of well-scrubbed potatoes and toss them with a little oil in a polythene bag, then sprinkle them over a non-stick baking (cookie) sheet. Cook the potato wedges on the hottest setting in the oven for about 30 minutes, turning once, until they are partly browned and just tender. Then reduce the oven setting and open the door for a while to reduce the temperature, ready for cooking the fish. As soon as the oven has cooled to the required temperature, place the fish in the oven and continue cooking both potato wedges and fish. Serve as a tasty alternative to deep-fried fish and chips, with lots of peas or baked beans.

Grilling (Broiling)

Grilling (broiling) is an excellent method for all fish and seafood, as long as delicate cuts are handled with care so that they are not broken. Steaks are more sturdy in texture than fillets, particularly firm swordfish and tuna. Thick fillets are suitable, especially when cut in small portions that can be turned easily. Whole fish, such as plaice, mackerel or herring, should be slashed diagonally across the skin in two or three places on each side to prevent the skin from bursting and to promote even cooking.

When cooking finer fillets – for example of whiting, plaice or red mullet – the trick is to support them adequately by placing on a flameproof dish or baking (cookie) sheet. Alternatively, line the grill (broiler) pan with foil. Grease the dish or foil well.

Chunks of firm fish and whole seafood, such as large tiger prawns (jumbo shrimp), can be threaded on metal skewers for grilling (broiling). These are best supported on greased foil or over a suitable baking (cookie) sheet or flameproof dish, otherwise the pieces of fish tend to become attached to the grill (broiler) rack during cooking

and it can then become quite difficult to turn the skewers.

Marinating for about 30 minutes or more is a good way of flavouring slightly bland fish, such as whiting, or moistening drier fish, such as swordfish. Herbs, spices and citrus rind and juice add flavour, while the juice also moistens. Oil, medium or dry white wine, cider or yogurt are all good for moistening dry ingredients. Remove the fish from large quantities of marinade before cooking, if necessary, reserving the latter.

Delicate shellfish can be grilled (broiled) on the half shell – oysters are good cooked this way. Clean and loosen the oysters, then trickle with a little melted butter and season lightly before grilling (broiling). Alternatively, poach oysters for about 1 minute, or slightly less, until they are just firm enough to handle, then drain them and wrap in lengths of thinly cut streaky bacon. Thread on to skewers before grilling. Similarly, wrap scallops in strips of bacon or Parma ham before grilling.

Peeled cooked prawns (shrimp) are delicious wrapped in bacon or ham, while raw prawns in the shell are ideal for grilling (broiling).

Brush the fish or seafood with a little oil before cooking, then turn it over halfway through cooking and brush with more oil or marinade before finishing.

Healthy Serving

- Grilled (broiled) fish and seafood is excellent on a mixed salad base – instead of the usual leafy mixture, try coarsely grated carrots, courgettes (zucchini), white radish and beetroot dressed with a little oil and vinegar.

- Fish brochettes – skewered pieces of white fish – are delicious in warm tortilla wraps or warm pitta bread. Add a tomato salsa or salad, or a bowl of diced cucumber and spring onions (scallions) in yogurt, to complement the brochettes.

- Serve small portions of grilled (broiled) skinless salmon fillet in toasted burger buns, with cucumber, lettuce and spring onions (scallions). Be sure to remove any stray bones from the fish before cooking it.

Cooking Times

These vary widely according to the shape, thickness, texture, size and type of fish or seafood. About 5–10 minutes on each side is enough for the majority of cooking under a preheated hot grill (broiler); allow up to 15 minutes at a slightly reduced, preheated moderate, temperature for extra thick or firm items.

Frying

Deep-frying is the method to avoid on all but rare occasions because, even when carried out at the right temperature and with the most careful of draining, it greatly increases the fat content of the food being cooked. If you do deep-fry fish for a once-in-a-blue-moon treat, then make sure you use fresh vegetable oil and that it is thoroughly heated to 190°C/375°F before the fish is added. Coat the fish with egg and breadcrumbs or dip it in batter before adding to the oil. Fry one or two items at a time so that the temperature of the oil does not drop too drastically. Drain well over the pan, then again on double-thick paper towels before serving.

Pan-frying does not have to be unhealthy. Be sure to buy a good-quality, heavy non-stick pan (skillet). Grease it lightly rather than cooking in generous puddles of fat. Use the minimum of sunflower oil and ensure the pan is hot before adding the fish or seafood.

Stir-frying is a useful method for fish and seafood with a more resilient texture – chunks of firm fish are suitable but thinner, delicate fillets break up too easily. Raw or cooked peeled prawns (shrimp), squid rings and scallops are all good for stir-frying.

Cooking Times

Frying times are fast: pan-fried fillets take 2–3 minutes on each side, while steaks take 3–7 minutes each side. Stir frying is particularly fast as long as the ingredients are cooked in small quantities.

Healthy Serving

- Complement this comparatively fat-rich method by serving plain boiled starchy ingredients – rice or new potatoes – as accompaniments. Add plenty of lightly cooked vegetables or salad.

- When stir-frying, include plenty of finely cut crisp vegetables along with a modest proportion of fish or seafood. Try fine green beans, thin sticks of carrot, sticks of celery, beansprouts, small broccoli florets and spring onions (scallions).

- Instead of serving oily sauces with pan-fried fish and seafood (such as the traditional tartare sauce), opt for a lighter accompaniment of low-fat Greek-style yogurt with snipped chives, or a herb salsa made from fresh basil, lime rind and juice and cucumber. Both are sufficiently tangy and full of flavour to enliven fried fish.

INTRODUCTION

INTRODUCTION

Achieving satisfaction, style and a sense of wellbeing seems to be essential these days, so it is just as well that seafood tastes fantastic and has a sophisticated image. Selecting fish and seafood fits in with fashion and contributes to the whole concept of making cooking and eating a pleasurable experience. The fact that it happens to be seriously good for you is the bonus that makes seafood supremely sensible for everyone – from tiny tots to the well matured; for style seekers or traditionalists, and for all of us somewhere in between.

Fish and seafood are savoured all over the world in dishes that are as varied as the cultures from which they originate. Delicately cooked or robustly dressed, fish can be prepared to suit all tastes, ages and pockets with the very minimum effort. While there is every opportunity for adventurous chefs to explore the full potential of seafood in finely tuned dishes created at master-class level, busy or less-confident cooks will appreciate the simple methods that work so well with fish dishes. Contemporary restaurants in cosmopolitan centres worldwide – from London to California and Sydney – have brought seafood to the creative forefront of vibrant fusion cooking, combining international flavours with simple pan-frying or grilling (broiling) with spectacular results that are the perfect inspiration for home cooks.

In countries where there is a long tradition of eating fish, the population has a lower rate of heart disease that is not entirely attributable to additional ingredients, such as an abundant use of vegetables or the choice of lower-fat cooking methods, as these vary widely in some cases.

INTRODUCTION

The traditional Japanese diet is rich in fish, especially fresh tuna, one of the oily fish that provides important omega-3 amino acids. Japanese cooking uses fish and seafood in many different dishes, including soups, noodle dishes, grills and casseroles. Deep-frying is used for some dishes, such as tempura, that present fish and seafood in an extremely light batter. Fish and seafood are also used as toppings or fillings for sushi, the moulded or shaped portions of vinegar-dressed rice. However, seafood is also appreciated to the extent that, when perfectly fresh, some fish are considered best served raw in sashimi. Sashimi is essentially a series of techniques for cutting fish into bite-size portions – they may be tissue-fine slices, perfect strips or neat wedges. The cuts are precise and important in making the most of the particular seafood or serving style. Wasabi, a root similar to horseradish but hotter and green in colour, is grated and added to soy sauce to make a dipping sauce for the sashimi. For anyone feeling nervous about sampling uncooked seafood for the first time, while tuna is excellent, the texture of raw squid can be rather more challenging.

Southeast Asian countries use fish and seafood in dishes that characteristically display the versatility of light cooking methods. Steaming, in particular, loses its bland Northern European image to become an aromatic and delicate method in the presence of ginger, lemon grass and spring onions (scallions). Braising and stir-frying are also popular Chinese methods for seafood.

The appreciation of raw fish is also evident in countries other than Japan; for example there is a South American dish called ceviche (or seviche). This consists of fish marinated in lime juice until it is firm and opaque. The acid in the juice firms the flesh of the seafood in the same way as cooking, while chillies, garlic, tomatoes or chopped fresh coriander (cilantro) may be added, with care, for additional flavour.

It is hardly surprising that seafood is popular throughout the Mediterranean, including Spain and Portugal, a region known for its low incidence of heart disease. Soups filled with fabulous mixed seafood are rich with vegetables and various seasonings; stewing and braising are widely used; and simple chargrilling (charbroiling) is especially popular for oily fish, such as sardines, or firm cuts of swordfish or tuna. Greece, Italy and the South of France all make extensive use of seafood in dishes that range from homely bakes to haûte cuisine. Turkey must be the country that is best known for perfecting the technique of making kebabs, with fish and seafood being popular ingredients along coastal regions, where mussels are grilled (broiled) on the half shell, with or without a tempting stuffing.

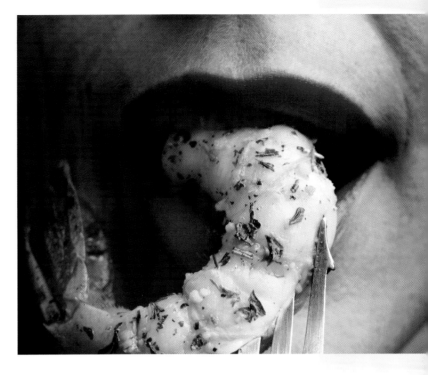

Northern Europe is not lacking in seafood traditions, with French haûte cuisine and British fish pies, simple pan-fried fish, oysters, mussels, kippers and, of course, fish and chips. They may not always be the best choice of cooking methods for healthy eating but, even so, these traditional dishes do ensure that everyday diets benefit from the valuable contribution seafood makes. And adjusting the cooking method or ingredients slightly is all that is needed to bring old favourites right up-to-date for healthy eating.

This book outlines the reasons why fish and seafood are beneficial to health in the context of a well-balanced diet. The opening chapters look at some of the ingredients that are available and the ways in which they can be prepared and cooked to best advantage. Then the recipe chapters provide a range of ideas for all occasions with the emphasis on balanced eating and practical cooking, mainly simple but with the occasional suggestion for something a little more adventurous. Hopefully, the background information will set your resolve to make the most of seafood, while the culinary suggestions will inspire and encourage you to stick to your new resolution.

Here's to good eating and great health!

SNACKS AND STARTERS

Refreshing Prawn Cocktails

With a creamy tomato dressing that is light and full flavoured, these prawn cocktails are deliciously different and far healthier than their predecessors of a few decades ago. Serve crisp wholemeal toast with the cocktails for a light first course, or generous chunks of crusty bread for a more substantial snack. Alternatively, pile the prawn mixture into baked potatoes and serve an extra large portion of salad leaves on the side.

Serves 4

2 tablespoons tomato purée (paste)

1 teaspoon caster sugar

½ teaspoon French mustard

salt and pepper

6 ripe tomatoes, peeled, de-seeded and chopped

3 tablespoons olive oil

4 spring onions (scallions), green parts only, chopped

2 tablespoons chopped parsley

grated zest of ½ lemon

250 ml/8 fl oz/1 cup fromage frais

400 g/14 oz peeled cooked prawns (shrimp)

50 g/2 oz watercress

50 g/2 oz rocket or lamb's lettuce

Use a whisk to mix the tomato purée, sugar and mustard. Season the mixture well, then whisk in the chopped tomatoes. Gradually whisk in the olive oil. Stir in the spring onions, parsley, lemon zest and fromage frais, then check the seasoning, adding more salt, pepper or sugar if required.

Pat the prawns dry on paper towels before adding them to the tomato mixture. Turn the prawns in the dressing, cover and leave to marinate in the refrigerator for at least 30 minutes before serving.

To serve, arrange the watercress and rocket or lamb's lettuce in small bowls or on large plates. Spoon the prawn mixture on top and serve at once.

Fresh Tuna and Olive Crostini

These delicious crostini are rich in good things, with omega-3 fatty acids from the tuna fish and mono-unsaturated fats from the olives and olive oil. Along with the positive contribution these fats make to a healthy diet, the garlic and spring onions (scallions) also assist in keeping unwanted levels of cholesterol under control.

Serves 4

4 garlic cloves, finely chopped
12 spring onions (scallions), chopped
2 tablespoons capers, drained and chopped (or rinse if salted, then drained and chopped)
100 g/3½ oz/1 cup pitted black olives, chopped
grated zest of 1 lemon and juice of ½ lemon
salt and pepper
2 tablespoons olive oil, plus extra for brushing bread
250 g/9 oz fresh tuna steak, diced
12 slices baguette or French stick
salad leaves and lemon wedges to serve

Mix the garlic, spring onions, capers, olives, lemon zest and juice. Stir in a little seasoning and then stir in the olive oil. Add the tuna steak, mix well and cover the bowl. Set aside to marinate for about 1 hour. The tuna can be left to marinate for several hours in the refrigerator.

Set the oven at 200°C, 400°F, Gas 6. Brush one side of the bread slices very lightly with olive oil, then place them, oiled sides down, in a large shallow dish or baking tin.

Stir the tuna mixture, then use a small spoon to divide it between the slices of bread. Spoon the juices evenly over the crostini, then bake them for 20 minutes, until crisp around the edges and succulent in the middle. Serve at once, with salad leaves and wedges of lemon.

Punchy Tuna and Anchovy Pâté

Tuna pâté is one of those dishes that traditionally contains large quantities of butter but this recipe is healthy and interesting, with mouth-watering flavour from anchovies and finely chopped onion. Serve with hearty chunks of crusty bread or toasted ciabatta, lots of crunchy fennel and handfuls of watercress sprigs to make a delicious lunch or supper. Use the pâté as a filling for baguettes or rolls, or spoon it into baked potatoes.

Serves 4

50 g/2 oz can anchovy fillets in olive oil
grated zest of 1 lemon and juice of ½ lemon
freshly ground black pepper
½ onion, finely chopped
1 celery stick (stalk), finely chopped
1 garlic clove, crushed
200 g/7 oz/⅔ cup low-fat soft cheese, eg curd cheese or quark
4 tablespoons chopped parsley
a little grated nutmeg

Pound the anchovies to a paste with the oil – do this in a large mortar, using a pestle, or by first mashing them with a fork, then pounding with the back of a mixing spoon. Alternatively, use a food processor to make the pâté.

Add the lemon zest and juice, plus a good grind of black pepper to the anchovy paste. Then work in the tuna to make a fairly smooth paste. Mix in the onion, celery, garlic, soft cheese and parsley. Season with a little nutmeg and turn out into a serving dish, or simply press the pâté down in the bowl and smooth the top with the back of a spoon.

Cover tightly and chill for at least 30 minutes before serving to allow the flavours to mingle.

Ginger-scented Salmon Tartlets

Filo pastry (paste) is quick and simple to use as long as it is kept covered with cling film (saran wrap) when you are not actually handling it to prevent it from drying out. A little zesty ginger brings a hint of lively freshness to salmon: serve the tartlets with a salad of cucumber, fennel and baby plum tomatoes for a healthy first course, or you can add plenty of new potatoes for a more substantial lunch.

Serves 4

1 tablespoon olive oil, plus extra for brushing

4 tablespoons snipped chives

3 tablespoons chopped fresh tarragon

2 tablespoons finely chopped fresh root ginger

1 tablespoon lemon juice

pinch of sugar

salt and pepper

350 g/12 oz salmon fillet, skinned and cut into small chunks

8 sheets of filo pastry (paste) 30 x 18 cm/12 x 7 in

6 tablespoons half-fat crème fraîche

Mix the olive oil, half the chives, 2 tablespoons tarragon, the ginger and lemon juice in a bowl. Season with a pinch of sugar, salt and pepper, then add the salmon and mix lightly. Cover and leave to marinate for 2–3 hours in the refrgerator.

Set the oven at 190°C/375°F/Gas 5. Cut each sheet of filo pastry across in half. Lightly grease four shallow tartlet dishes or Yorkshire pudding tins with olive oil. Brush a piece of filo pastry with a little olive oil and place it, oiled side down, in one tin. Crumple the base slightly and leave the corners sticking up. Brush another piece of filo with a little olive oil and place it on top of the first, crumpling it and arranging it so that the points do not line up with those of the bottom piece of pastry. Repeat with the remaining pastry and tins.

Stir the marinated salmon, then divide it between the tartlets, piling the pieces neatly in the middle. Spoon the herbs and any juice in the bowl over the salmon and bake for about 25 minutes, until the pastry is crisp and golden and the salmon is cooked and browned in places on top.

Meanwhile, mix the remaining chives and tarragon into the crème fraîche. Carefully lift the tartlets from the tins and place them on plates. Top each with a little herb cream and serve at once.

Tarragon Pancakes with Spicy Anchovy Dressing and Carrot and Courgette Salad

Traditionally, these thick little British pancakes, known as pikelets or drop scones, are served with butter and sugar as a sweet treat. This savoury version is deliciously different and great for a first course or snack. Served with generous helpings of mixed leaf salad topped with coarsely grated carrot and courgette (zucchini), these pancakes are also a healthy choice for a slightly special lunch.

Serves 4

50 g/2 oz can anchovy fillets in olive oil
¼ teaspoon ground mace
¼ teaspoon ground allspice
¼ teaspoon ground ginger
freshly ground black pepper
1 tablespoon tomato purée (paste)
4 tablespoons olive oil
squeeze of lemon juice
4 ripe tomatoes, peeled, de-seeded and chopped

Tarragon Pancakes
125 g/4½ oz/1¼ cups self-raising flour (all-purpose flour with baking powder)
½ teaspoons dried tarragon
1 egg
1 tablespoon olive oil
150 ml/¼ pint/⅔ cup milk
sunflower oil for cooking

Carrot and Courgette Salad
4 small to medium carrots, coarsely grated
4 small courgettes (zucchini), coarsely grated
2 spring onions (scallions), chopped
squeeze of lemon juice
generous mixed leaf salad

Using a food processor or mortar and pestle, purée the anchovy fillets to a paste with the oil from the can, the mace, allspice, ginger and a generous seasoning of black pepper. Mix in the tomato purée, then gradually work in the olive oil and a little lemon juice. Stir in the tomatoes and transfer to a small saucepan; set side.

Prepare the salad before making the pancakes. Mix the carrots, courgettes and spring onions with a little lemon juice. Cover and set aside.

To make the pancakes, place the flour in a bowl and stir in the tarragon. Make a well in the middle, then add the egg and the oil. Pour in a little of the milk and then gradually beat it into the egg and oil. Continue beating, gradually working in the flour and adding the remaining milk a little at a time to make a smooth, thick batter.

Grease a flat griddle or heavy non-stick frying pan (skillet) with a little sunflower oil, then heat over medium heat. Use a dessertspoon to pour some batter on to the hot pan: hold the spoon quite high above the pan as you pour the batter and it will drop into a neat round shape. Cook the batter until the underside has set and browned and the top surface is still moist, and covered with small bursting bubbles. Turn the pancake and cook the second side. Reduce or increase the heat under the pan so that there is enough time

for the batter to bubble and set before the underneath is overcooked. Repeat with the remaining batter, cooking several pancakes at once. Keep the pancakes hot in a warm oven, in a dish lined with paper towels and covered with foil until all the batter is cooked.

Meanwhile, heat the anchovy dressing gently until hot, but not bubbling furiously. Arrange the mixed salad leaves on four large plates, then pile the grated salad on top. Arrange the hot pancakes overlapping on the plates. Stir the anchovy dressing well and spoon it over the pancakes. Serve at once.

Preheat the grill (broiler) on the hottest setting. Mash the sardines with the oil from the can, then mix in the mustard, spring onions, garlic and lemon zest. Add salt and pepper to taste.

Toast the bread on one side, turn the slices and very lightly toast the second side until they are just beginning to brown. Divide the sardine mixture between the slices of toast and spread it evenly, right up to their edges. Grill (broil) until well browned, placing the grill (broiler) pan quite far away from the heat source to avoid burning the topping before it is hot.

Top with the wild rocket and halved cherry tomatoes, or serve this salad to one side on the same plate as the toasties. Add a wedge or two of lemon to each slice, so that the juice can be squeezed over to taste, and serve at once.

Sardine Toasties with Cherry Tomatoes, Rocket and Lemon

This contemporary take on sardines on toast is refreshingly different. Cut extra-thick slices of wholemeal bread to mop up the full flavour of the sardine topping. Try a crisp juicy apple to follow for both flavour and food value.

Serves 4

120 g/4¼ oz can sardines in olive oil
1 teaspoon wholegrain mustard
2 spring onions (scallions), chopped
1 garlic clove, crushed
grated zest of ½ lemon
salt and pepper
4 very thick slices wholemeal bread
50 g/2 oz wild rocket
16 cherry tomatoes, halved
lemon wedges to serve

Tuna Tortilla with Red Pepper Salsa

This is good hot, warm or cold. Serve slim wedges for a stylish starter or hearty chunks for lunch; it is also ideal picnic fare.

Serves 4-6

700 g/1lb 9 oz salad potatoes or small new potatoes

2 large onions, chopped

2 tablespoons olive oil

6 eggs

6 tablespoons milk

good handful of parsley, chopped

200 g/7 oz can tuna in brine, drained and flaked

Red (Bell) Pepper Salsa

1 tablespoon fennel seeds

2 tablespoons olive oil

½ teaspoon paprika

2 tablespoons balsamic vinegar

2 teaspoons caster sugar

2 red (bell) peppers, cores removed, and finely diced

1 fresh red chilli, de-seeded and chopped (optional)

2 tomatoes, chopped

4 spring onions (scallions), chopped

2 garlic cloves, finely chopped

salt and pepper

Make the salsa in advance, if possible, so that the ingredients have time to marinate and the flavours develop. Place the fennel seeds, olive oil and paprika in a small saucepan and heat gently until the seeds begin to sizzle lightly. Remove from the heat and whisk in the balsamic vinegar and sugar. Stir in the peppers, chilli (if using), tomatoes, spring onions and garlic. Taste for seasoning and add salt and pepper as required. Transfer to a serving bowl, cover and leave to marinate.

Cook the potatoes in boiling, lightly salted water for about 15 minutes, or until just tender. Drain and cut into chunks. Meanwhile, cook the onions in the olive oil in a large frying pan (skillet) over fairly gentle heat for about 20 minutes or until they are softened but not browned.

Add the potatoes and to onions and mix well. Whisk the eggs with the milk and seasoning. Add the parsley and tuna and mix lightly. Pour the tuna mixture evenly over the potatoes and cook very gently for 30–40 minutes, until the egg has set. If the heat is too high, the underneath will burn before the middle is set. The egg should be just set on top. Preheat the grill (broiler) and hold the pan under it to brown the top of the tortilla.

Allow the tortilla to stand for about 15 minutes before cutting it into portions and serving with the salsa.

SOUPS AND STEWS

Prawn, Pepper and Sweetcorn Soup

A twist of lime and a hint of chilli and coriander (cilantro) bring a zing to this golden soup. With lots of onion and yellow (bell) pepper as well as the prawns (shrimp), the soup is also full of vitamin goodness. Serve with bread rolls or warm, puffy individual nan bread to make a hearty lunch.

Serves 6

2 onions, chopped
2 garlic cloves, crushed
1 fresh green chilli, de-seeded and chopped
2 yellow (bell) peppers, cores removed and finely diced
2 tablespoons sunflower oil
450 g/1 lb sweetcorn (corn) kernels, frozen or fresh
400 g/14 oz peeled cooked prawns (shrimp)
1.2 litres/2 pints/5 cups chicken stock
salt and pepper
grated zest of 1 lime and juice of ½ lime
chopped fresh coriander (cilantro) leaves

Cook the onions, garlic, chilli and peppers in the oil in a large covered saucepan for about 15 minutes, stirring occasionally, until the onions are softened but not browned. Add the sweetcorn and a third of the prawns, then pour in the stock and add a little seasoning. Bring to the boil. Reduce the heat, cover the pan and simmer the soup for 20 minutes.

Purée the soup coarsely in a blender, or use a hand-held blender or food processor, then return it to the pan. Reheat the soup until just boiling, then taste for seasoning and reduce the heat before adding the remaining prawns, lime zest and juice. Cook gently for a few minutes until the prawns are heated. Stir in some chopped fresh coriander and serve at once.

Smoked Fish Chowder

Select undyed smoked fish for this delicious, vegetable-rich chowder.

Serves 4

2 bay leaves

4 large parsley sprigs

2 thyme sprigs

1 large onion, chopped

1 fennel bulb, roughly chopped

4 celery sticks (stalks), diced

4 carrots, diced

2 tablespoons olive oil

salt and pepper

2 large potatoes, cut into 1 cm/½ in cubes

1.12 litres/2 pints/5 cups fish or chicken stock

2 small courgettes (zucchini), diced

700 g/1lb 9 oz smoked haddock (blue cod/hoki) fillet, skinned and cut into chunks

4 tablespoons chopped parsley

Tie the bay leaves, parsley and thyme together with a piece of string to make a bouquet garni. Place the onion, fennel, celery, carrots and bouquet garni in a large saucepan with the olive oil. Add a little seasoning and mix well. Cover the pan and cook over medium heat for about 20 minutes, stirring occasionally, until the onion has softened slightly and the other vegetables are lightly cooked.

Add the potatoes and pour in the stock, then bring to the boil. Reduce the heat so that the soup simmers gently and cover the pan. Cook for 30 minutes. Add the courgettes and haddock, then cook gently for a further 10 minutes until the chunks of fish are firm and opaque. Taste for seasoning and add the parsley before serving.

Seafood Broth with Noodles and Broccoli

Fresh coriander (cilantro) leaves and fabulous basil taste brilliant together in this light broth. With succulent fish, slightly crisp vegetables and satisfying noodles it is a healthy choice for a light lunch or supper.

Serves 4

2 tablespoons dry sherry
1 tablespoon light soy sauce
3 tablespoons chopped fresh coriander (cilantro) leaves
4 spring onions (scallions), chopped
500 g/1 lb 2 oz skinless white fish fillet,
cut into 1 cm/½ in pieces
1.2 litres/2 pints/5 cups good fish or chicken stock
1 garlic clove, finely chopped
2 carrots, diced
450 g/1 lb broccoli, cut into small florets
225 g/8 oz dried Chinese egg noodles
salt and pepper
handful of tender basil sprigs

Mix the sherry, soy sauce, coriander and 2 of the chopped spring onions in a bowl. Add the fish and turn the pieces in the seasoning mixture until well coated. Cover and leave to marinate for 1–3 hours before cooking.

Pour the stock into a large saucepan. Add the carrots and remaining spring onions, and bring to the boil. Simmer for 2 minutes, then add the broccoli and simmer for 2 minutes. Add the noodles and bring the broth back to a full boil.

Reduce the temperature so that the soup barely simmers and add the fish, scraping in all the marinade from the bowl. Season the broth lightly and simmer gently for 5 minutes, until the noodles are just tender and the fish is cooked. Taste the broth and add more salt and pepper if necessary.

Remove the pan from the heat and use scissors to shred the basil into the broth. Serve immediately.

Seafood Soup with Rice and Pesto

This is hearty and wholesome, full of seafood and vegetable goodness, and laced with punchy pesto. Serve great chunks or wedges of country style bread to complement the soup and make a substantial meal.

Serves 4

2 tablespoons olive oil

1 large onion, chopped

1 fennel bulb, chopped

2 carrots, diced

2 garlic cloves, crushed

2 bay leaves

2 thyme sprigs

grated zest of 1 lemon

salt and pepper

400 g/14 oz can chopped tomatoes

900 ml/1½ pints/3¾ cups fish or chicken stock

100 g/3½ oz/½ cup uncooked long-grain rice

250 g/9 oz tuna fillet, cut into 1 cm/½ in dice

350 g/12 oz peeled cooked tiger prawns (jumbo shrimp)

350 g/12 oz shelled cooked mussels

home-made or bought pesto to serve

Heat the oil for a few seconds in a large saucepan. Add the onion, fennel, carrots, garlic, bay leaves, thyme sprigs and lemon zest. Season the mixture lightly and stir well, then cover and cook over medium heat for 20 minutes, until the vegetables are tender but not browned.

Pour in the tomatoes with the juice from the can and the stock. Bring to the boil, then reduce the heat and cover the pan. Simmer the soup for 15 minutes. Stir in the rice and continue simmering for a further 15 minutes or until the rice is cooked.

Taste the soup and adjust the seasoning before adding the tuna. Simmer for 2 minutes to cook the small pieces of tuna, then add the cooked prawns and mussels. Heat the prawns and mussels gently without allowing the soup to boil. Taste for seasoning and ladle the soup into bowls. Add a little pesto to each portion and offer more separately.

Salmon Broth with Soup Pasta

The rich flavour of salmon is excellent in light broth, especially with pasta. Fine green beans and thin strips of red (bell) pepper are delicious and nutritious with the fish.

Serves 4

2 tablespoons olive oil

450 g/1 lb salmon fillet, skinned and cut into 4 equal pieces

1 large onion, chopped

1 bay leaf

2 carrots, finely diced

2 celery sticks (stalks), finely diced

long strip of pared lemon peel

salt and pepper

1 red (bell) pepper, cored and cut into short fine strips

100 ml/4 fl oz/⅓ cup dry white wine

900 ml/1½ pints/3¾ cups fish or chicken stock

75 g/3 oz small soup pasta shapes

175 g/6 oz fine green beans, cut into short lengths

4 tablespoons chopped fresh dill (dill weed)

Heat the oil in a large non-stick frying pan (skillet). Cook the pieces of salmon fillet until lightly browned on each side and just cooked. Use a fish slice to transfer the pieces of fish to a plate and set aside.

Add the onion, bay leaf, carrots, celery and lemon peel to the oil remaining in the pan. Sprinkle with seasoning and cook, stirring often, for about 15 minutes, until the vegetables are softened slightly, but not browned. Add the red pepper and cook for 2-3 minutes, stirring, to soften it slightly. Then pour in the wine and bring to the boil. Boil for 2 minutes.

Pour the contents of the frying pan (skillet) into a large saucepan, scraping out all the cooking juices. Add the stock and bring to the boil. Then add the soup pasta and green beans and simmer for about 5 minutes, or for the time suggested on the pasta packet. Taste and adjust the seasoning, then stir in the dill.

Meanwhile, cut the salmon into bite-sized chunks and divide between four large, warmed bowls. Ladle the soup into the bowls and serve at once.

Spicy Fish Soup

Warm, mild spices bring a gentle glow to this simple soup made with white fish, such as hoki, haddock or cod; salmon is also suitable. Sugarsnap peas and shredded spinach contrast well with the fish and spices. Offer crisp popadoms or warm nan bread with the soup.

Serves 4

2 tablespoons sunflower oil

I large onion, chopped

2 carrots, diced

2 celery sticks (stalks), diced

3 garlic cloves, crushed

25 g/I oz fresh ginger root, peeled and finely chopped

I cinnamon stick

salt and pepper

2 teaspoons ground coriander (cilantro)

½ teaspoon ground turmeric

900 ml/1½ pints/3¾ cups fish stock

225 g/8 oz sugarsnap peas, sliced at an angle

700 g/I lb 9 oz white fish fillet, skinned and cut into chunks

225 g/8 oz young spinach, finely shredded

a little chopped fresh coriander (cilantro)

4–6 tablespoons single (light) cream, to serve (optional)

Heat the oil in a large saucepan and add the onion, carrots, celery, garlic, ginger and cinnamon stick. Add a little salt and pepper, then cook, stirring occasionally, for about 15 minutes, or until the onion has softened. Stir in the coriander and turmeric and cook for about 30 seconds before pouring in the fish stock. Bring to the boil, reduce the heat and cover the pan. Simmer the soup gently for 30 minutes.

Add the sugarsnap peas and fish, cover the pan and continue simmering gently for 5 minutes or until the peas and fish are cooked. Stir in the spinach and cook briefly until it has wilted and reduced. Taste the soup for seasoning and sprinkle in a little chopped fresh coriander. Ladle the soup into warm bowls and trickle a little cream into each portion, if liked. Serve at once.

Onion and Tomato Soup with Tuna Crostini

This full-flavoured soup is served with freshly cooked tuna crostini floating on top to make a satisfying and healthy meal. Drained canned tuna can be used instead of the fresh fish for a simple and economical soup.

Serves 4

2 tablespoons sunflower oil
6 large onions, halved and thinly sliced
1 teaspoon sugar
2 bay leaves
3–4 large fresh oregano, marjoram or thyme sprigs
1 kg/2 lb ripe tomatoes, peeled, de-seeded and diced
salt and pepper
paprika
2 tablespoons tomato purée (paste)
1.2 litres/2 pints/5 cups chicken or vegetable stock
150 ml/¼ pint/⅔ cup dry sherry

Tuna Crostini
225 g/ 8 oz tuna steak, finely diced
2 spring onions (scallions), chopped
2 garlic cloves, chopped
grated zest of ½ orange
150 g/5 oz/1⅓ cups mozzarella cheese, finely diced
12 thick slices of baguette or French stick, cut at an angle

Heat the sunflower oil in a large, heavy-bottomed saucepan. Add the onions and stir well, then cover the pan and cook, stirring occasionally, for about 30 minutes or until the onions are thoroughly softened. Sprinkle the sugar over the onions and continue to cook, uncovered, for a further 10–15 minutes, or until the onions are browned.

Add the bay leaves, herb sprigs and tomatoes to the onions. Season well with salt and pepper, and add a good sprinkling of paprika. Cook for a minute or so before adding the tomato purée, stock and sherry. Bring to the boil, reduce the heat and cover the pan. Simmer the soup for 30 minutes.

To make the crostini, mix the tuna, spring onions, garlic, orange zest and mozzarella in a bowl, adding seasoning to taste. Toast the slices of bread on one side. Divide the tuna mixture between the bread slices, placing it on the untoasted sides.

Heat the grill (broiler) to a medium setting and cook the tuna crostini until the topping is bubbling and browned. Ladle the soup into warmed bowls and float the freshly cooked crostini on top. Serve at once.

Mussel, Fennel and Leek Soup

A little bacon tastes fabulous with mussels and vegetables in this soup, which is bursting with flavour. Serve plenty of warm, crusty bread to mop up every last drop of delicious liquid.

Serves 4-6

2 tablespoons olive oil
2 bay leaves
2 rindless bacon rashers (slices), diced
1 onion, finely chopped
1 celery stick (stalk), finely chopped
1 carrot, finely chopped
salt and pepper
150 ml/¼ pint/⅔ cup dry white wine
1 kg/2¼ lb mussels, scrubbed and beards removed
2 fennel bulbs, chopped
450 g/1 lb leeks, chopped
2 potatoes, diced
900 ml/1½ pints/3¾ cups fish stock
150 ml/¼ pint/⅔ cup crème fraîche
4 tablespoons chopped parsley

Place 1 tablespoon of the olive oil in a large saucepan. Add the bay leaves, bacon, onion, celery and carrot. Sprinkle with a little seasoning and heat, stirring, until the mixture begins to sizzle lightly. Cover the pan and cook for 15 minutes, stirring occasionally, until the onion has softened and the bacon is cooked.

Pour in the wine and bring to the boil, then add the mussels. Cover the pan and reduce the heat to medium, if necessary, so that the liquid does not boil too rapidly. Cook for 5–7 minutes or until the mussels have opened.

Shake the pan occasionally to ensure that the mussels cook evenly.

Remove the pan from the heat. Shell the mussels, discarding any that have not opened, pouring the liquor from the shells back into the pan. Place the mussels in a bowl and set aside. Pour the liquor and vegetables from the pan into a bowl or jug and set aside.

Pour the remaining oil into the pan and add the fennel and leeks. Cover and cook, stirring occasionally, for about 15 minutes, or until the leeks have softened. Add the potatoes and pour in the reserved cooking liquid from the mussels. Pour in the stock and bring to the boil. Reduce the heat, cover the pan and simmer for 30 minutes.

Taste the soup for seasoning before adding the cooked mussels. Heat gently, without boiling, for a few seconds. Do not cook the mussels or they will toughen. Remove the pan from the heat and stir in the crème fraîche and parsley. Serve at once.

Using Cooked Mussels

Cooked mussels in their shells, sold vacuum-packed with their cooking liquor can be used if preferred. Cook the bacon and vegetable mixture with the fennel and leeks, and add the wine with the stock. Follow the packet instructions for reheating the mussels, shell them and add them to the soup at the end of cooking with their liquor.

Mackerel Rolls Braised in Vegetable Ragoût

Tomatoes, onions and (bell) peppers make a rich sauce for full-flavoured mackerel. Other fish, such as tuna, swordfish or white fish, can be used instead, cut in steaks or thick portions of fillet instead of arranged in rolls. Serve rice or couscous with the mackerel and vegetables.

Serves 4

2 tablespoons olive oil
2 garlic cloves, crushed
I large onion, chopped
I large green (bell) pepper, cored, halved and diced
I large red (bell) pepper, cored, halved and diced
salt and pepper
4 courgettes (zucchini), cut into 1.5 cm/¾ in chunks
600 g/I lb 5 oz tomatoes, peeled and diced
150 ml/¼ pint/⅔ cup dry cider
2 teaspoons sugar
8 small mackerel fillets
3 tablespoons capers, chopped
6 tablespoons chopped fresh dill (dill weed)
I teaspoon finely chopped fresh rosemary

Set the oven at 200°C, 400°F, Gas 6. Heat the oil in a large frying pan (skillet) and add the garlic, onion, red and green peppers with a little seasoning. Cook, stirring frequently, for 15 minutes, then add the courgettes and cook, stirring, for about 2 minutes. Stir in the tomatoes, cider and sugar and bring to the boil. Transfer to an ovenproof casserole, cover and cook in the oven for 20 minutes.

Meanwhile, remove any remaining bones from the mackerel fillets and lay the fish skin sides down on a board. Mix the capers, dill and rosemary with seasoning, then divide this evenly between the fillets, sprinkling it evenly over them. Roll up the fillets from the wide end and secure with wooden cocktail sticks.

Remove the casserole from the oven and stir the vegetables. Taste for seasoning, adding more salt and pepper, if necessary. Arrange the mackerel rolls in the casserole, nestling them down into the vegetables. Cover and continue to cook for a further 30 minutes, until the mackerel rolls are cooked through. Serve the rolls and ragoût piping hot.

Swordfish with Coconut, Ginger and Lemon Grass

A little coconut enriches this zingy fish casserole, spiced with ginger and aromatic lemon grass. Serve with stir-fried vegetables and fragrant Thai rice or basmati rice.

Serve 4

2 tablespoons sunflower oil
1 green chilli, de-seeded and chopped
8–10 spring onions (scallions), cut into short fine strips
2 carrots, cut into short fine strips
25 g/1 oz fresh ginger root, peeled and finely chopped
2 garlic cloves, finely chopped
2 lemon grass stems
½ teaspoons ground turmeric
300 ml/½ pint/1¼ cups fish or chicken stock
300 ml/½ pint/1¼ cups coconut milk
salt and pepper
700 g/1 lb 9 oz swordfish steak, cut into 2.5 cm/1 in cubes
200 g/7 oz mangetout (snow) peas, cut at an angle into thirds
chopped fresh coriander (cilantro) leaves

Heat the sunflower oil in a large flameproof casserole. Add the chilli, spring onions, carrots, ginger, garlic and lemon grass. Cook for 2–3 minutes, stirring, then add the turmeric and continue to cook for a further 2–3 minutes.

Pour in the stock and coconut milk with a generous sprinkling of seasoning and bring to the boil. Reduce the heat and simmer for 15 minutes. Taste the sauce and add a little seasoning if necessary. Then add the swordfish and simmer for a further 10 minutes. Add the mangetout and simmer for 5 minutes. Sprinkle with a little chopped fresh coriander leaves before serving.

Halibut with Cucumber and Pernod

This traditional-style recipe is ideal for all types of white fish as well as salmon or trout. Serve new potatoes or fluffy mash and a selection of vegetables to complete the main course.

Serves 4

25 g/1 oz/2 tablespoons butter
1 small onion, finely chopped
1 small carrot, finely diced
1 cucumber, peeled, de-seeded and diced
1 bay leaf
2 thyme sprigs
strip of pared lemon peel
salt and pepper
2 teaspoons plain (all-purpose) flour
300 ml/½ pint/1¼ cups fish stock
4 portions of halibut steak, about 150 g/5 oz each
6 tablespoons Pernod (or other aniseed-flavoured spirit or liqueur)
4 tablespoons single (light) cream

Garnish
lemon slices
cucumber slices
thyme sprigs

Melt the butter in a large flameproof casserole or deep frying pan (skillet) with a lid. Add the onion, carrot, cucumber, bay leaf, thyme and lemon peel. Sprinkle with a little seasoning, cover and cook gently for 20 minutes, or until the vegetables are softened.

Stir in the flour and pour in the fish stock, then bring to the boil, stirring. Cover and simmer for 10 minutes. Add the halibut to the pan, arranging the portions neatly and spooning the sauce over them. Cover and simmer gently for about 15 minutes or until the fish is cooked.

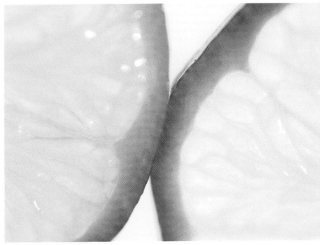

Meanwhile, heat a dish. Use a slotted spoon to transfer the halibut to the dish, cover and keep warm. Add the Pernod to the sauce and boil hard until reduced by half, stirring frequently. Discard the herbs and lemon peel from the sauce. Remove the pan from the heat before stirring in the cream, then taste for seasoning. Divide the sauce between four warm plates and arrange the halibut portions on top. Garnish with lemon, cucumber and thyme and serve at once.

STEAMED TO PERFECTION

Moules Marinière

Cooked in the steam from simmering wine with vegetables, herbs and garlic, these mussels have the most fabulous flavour. Serve plenty of crusty bread to mop up every last drop of the delicious cooking liquor and provide separate bowls for holding the empty mussel shells.

Serves 4

2 tablespoons olive oil
2 bay leaves
2 thyme sprigs
3 parsley sprigs
3 shallots, finely chopped
2 celery sticks (stalks), finely chopped
1 carrot, finely chopped
salt and pepper
250 ml/8 fl oz/1 cup dry white wine
1 kg/2¼ lb mussels, scrubbed and beards removed
good handful of parsley, chopped

Place the olive oil in a large saucepan or stockpot and heat gently. Tie the bay leaves, thyme and parsley together, then add to the pan with the shallots, celery and carrot. Sprinkle with a little seasoning and stir well. Cover and cook for 10 minutes, stirring occasionally. Pour in the wine and bring to the boil, then reduce the heat, cover the pan and simmer gently for 15 minutes.

Bring the liquid back to the boil, add the mussels. Cover the pan and reduce the heat to medium, so that the liquid does not boil too rapidly. Cook for 5–7 minutes or until the mussels have opened. Shake the pan occasionally to ensure that the mussels cook evenly.

Meanwhile, place a colander or strainer over a large bowl and tip the mussels with their liquor into it. Transfer mussels to a heated bowl, then cover tightly with foil or a plate. Rinse the pan if there is any grit or sand in the bottom, then pour the cooking liquor back into it. Bring to a full boil and boil rapidly until slightly reduced. Taste and adjust the seasoning, then add the chopped parsley.

Divide the mussels between four warmed bowls, discarding any that have not opened. Ladle the cooking liquor over them and serve immediately.

Steamed Prawns with Ginger and Spring Onions

Serve fragrant Thai jasmine rice and mixed stir-fried vegetables – such as carrots, broccoli, green beans and bean sprouts – with the steamed prawns (shrimp) to make a nutritious, light meal.

Serves 4

100 ml/4 fl oz/½ cup sake or dry sherry
2 slices fresh ginger root, peeled and finely shredded
1 garlic clove, finely chopped
700 g/1 lb 9 oz peeled raw tiger prawns (jumbo shrimp)
8 spring onions (scallions), finely shredded
2 tablespoons light soy sauce
2 large carrots
225 g/ 8 oz mangetout (snow) peas

In a small saucepan, heat the sake or dry sherry with the ginger and garlic until boiling. Boil until reduced by half, leaving a small amount of liquid in the pan with the ginger and garlic. Remove from the heat and leave to cool.

Place the prawns in a bowl and add the spring onions. Pour in the soy sauce and cooled sake or sherry, scraping all the ginger and garlic out of the pan. Mix well, cover and leave to marinate for 2–3 hours before cooking.

Trim and peel the carrots, then use a vegetable peeler to pare them into ribbons. Cut the mangetout peas across at a slant in half or into thirds, depending on size, and mix them with the carrot ribbons in a heatproof bowl that will fit in a steamer. Top the vegetables with the prawns and their marinade, scraping every last bit over them. Cover with foil, pinching it tightly around the rim of the bowl.

Bring to the boil a large pan of water with a steamer over it. Place the heatproof bowl in the steamer and cook over the boiling water for 15 minutes – or until the prawns are pink and just cooked. Serve at once.

Aromatic Steamed Salmon with Cool Herb Sauce

Steaming is an excellent method of cooking salmon, either whole, in large fillets or steaks. These steaks are good hot or cold, with new potatoes and salad or vegetables.

Serves 4

1 lemon
1.2 litres/2 pints/5 cups water
1 onion, thinly sliced
3 bay leaves
6 thyme sprigs
6 rosemary sprigs
1 tablespoon whole black peppercorns
salt
4 salmon steaks, skinned
sunflower oil for greasing

Cool Herb Sauce
3 tablespoons chopped parsley
3 tablespoons snipped chives
300 ml/½ pint/1¼ cups fromage frais
pinch of caster sugar

Grate the zest off about half the lemon and set it aside. Thinly slice the rest of the lemon and place it in a steamer base. Pour in the water and add the onion, bay leaves, thyme and rosemary sprigs, peppercorns and a pinch of salt. Cover and heat gently until boiling. Boil for 5 minutes, then remove from the heat and leave to cool completely.

If necessary, cut four small squares of non-stick baking parchment or foil on which to place the salmon steaks in the steamer. Grease the paper or foil, if using, or the steamer. Place the salmon steaks in the steamer. Bring the water and aromatics to the boil, then place the steamer over the pan and cook the salmon for 15 minutes.

Meanwhile, mix the parsley, chives and reserved lemon zest into the fromage frais. Add the sugar, season with a little salt, if liked, and stir well. Transfer the salmon steaks to warm plates and top each with a little of the herb sauce. Serve at once, offering the remaining herb sauce separately.

Note
Strain the liquid and discard the aromatics, then use it later as cooking liquor for fish, or in fish soup.

Basil-filled Trout in Lettuce Wraps

Serve creamy mashed potatoes, crisp green beans and a salad of cherry tomatoes to complement this aromatic fish dish and make a fabulously healthy main course.

Serves 4

12 Cos lettuce leaves
4 small trout, heads and tails removed, and boned
40 g/1½ oz/3 tablespoons butter, melted
3 tablespoons olive oil
1 tablespoon lemon juice
4 large basil sprigs
salt and pepper
lemon wedges to serve

Bring a large saucepan of water to the boil. Add the Cos lettuce leaves, bring back to the boil and drain immediately. Pat the lettuce leaves dry on clean tea-towels or paper towels.

Check the opened-out trout and remove any remaining bones. Whisk the butter, oil and lemon juice together. Overlap 3 lettuce leaves on a board and place 1 trout on top, skin side down. Brush with some of the butter mixture, then snip 1 basil sprig over the fish. Season well and fold the fish over to close it around the basil. Wrap the lettuce around the trout, folding the ends over to seal in it. Repeat with the remaining ingredients, reserving the remaining butter mixture.

Place the trout in a steamer and cook over boiling water for 20 minutes. Meanwhile, heat the remaining butter and oil mixture. Transfer the cooked trout to warm plates and drizzle the butter and oil over the top. Serve at once.

Vine-leaf steamed Hake with Rocket and Grape Salad

Hake is a firm fish with a delicate, slightly nutty flavour. Vaguely tangy vine leaves complement the hake while protecting it and keeping it succulent during steaming.

Serves 4

12 vine leaves (fresh, canned or vacuum packed)
4 (175 g/6 oz) portions hake fillet
3 tablespoons olive oil
salt and pepper
4 bay leaves
1 Little Gem lettuce heart, shredded
100 g/4 oz rocket
100 g/4 oz/1 cup seedless green grapes, halved
2 spring onions (scallions), chopped
1 teaspoon Dijon mustard
1 teaspoon caster sugar
1 tablespoon cider vinegar

Cook the vine leaves in boiling water for 5 minutes, drain well and mop on paper towels. Overlap 3 vine leaves and place a portion of fish on top. Brush the fish lightly with olive oil, season with salt and pepper and top with a bay leaf, crumpling the leaf to release its aroma and flavour. Wrap the fish in the vine leaves and place, fold underneath, in a steamer. Repeat with the remaining vine leaves, fish and bay leaves.

Bring the steamer base of water to the boil and steam the fish packages for 25 minutes. While the fish is steaming, mix the lettuce and rocket with the grapes and spring onions. Set aside.

Whisk the mustard, caster sugar, cider vinegar and a generous sprinkling of seasoning together in a small bowl until the sugar has dissolved. Whisk in the remaining olive oil. Arrange the fish in vine leaves on warmed plates. Arrange the salad on the plates, drizzle the dressing over and serve.

Separate the leek slices into rings and place them in an even layer in a steamer. Arrange the carrots in an even layer on top. Trim the fish fillets, removing any bits of membrane or remains of fins. Lay a fillet skin side down and season well. Sprinkle the leaves from 1 tarragon sprig over the flesh, then fold the fillet in half and place on top of the vegetables. Repeat with the remaining fillets. Steam the vegetables and fish over boiling water for about 20 minutes, or until vegetables and fish are cooked.

Tarragon Fillets with Leeks and Carrots in Orange Dressing

This recipe is ideal for fine-textured, delicate fish, such as plaice (flounder), megrim or lemon sole (English sole). To make the most of complementary ingredients – slightly sweet carrots with a sharp tinge of orange and aromatic tarragon – the cooking method is as simple as can be. Serve with couscous or new potatoes and a generous salad of watercress and baby spinach with segments of fresh orange.

Meanwhile, grate the zest from about half the orange, then squeeze out all its juice. Place zest and juice in a small saucepan and whisk in seasoning, with the mustard and olive oil. Bring to the boil, whisking all the time, and cook for 1 minute. Remove from the heat and cool slightly, then taste for seasoning, adding more salt, pepper, sugar or mustard to taste.

Arrange the fish fillets and vegetables on warm plates and spoon the orange dressing over. Serve immediately.

Serves 4

2 leeks, thinly sliced
500 g/1 lb 2 oz carrots, thinly sliced
4 large pale-skinned plaice fillets
salt and pepper
4 tarragon sprigs

Orange Dressing

1 large orange
½ teaspoon caster sugar
½ teaspoon wholegrain mustard
4 tablespoons olive oil

Hot Salmon and Potato Salad

This dream dish is good for the mind, body and image – it tastes terrific and is ever so stylish as well as being packed with great nutrients. Based on ample portions, it all adds up to a substantial meal. You can vary the salad base to make the best of those available and to include your favourite leaves – try lamb's lettuce, radicchio and lollo biondo or rosso, for example.

Serves 4

4 boneless, skinless salmon steaks
700 g/1 lb 9 oz small salad potatoes or new potatoes
salt and pepper
1 Cos lettuce heart, shredded
100 g/4 oz watercress
100 g/4 oz baby spinach leaves
handful or packet of parsley sprigs
handful or packet of dill (dill weed) sprigs
handful of chives, finely snipped
1 teaspoon wholegrain mustard
1 teaspoon caster sugar
grated zest of 1 lemon and juice of ½ lemon
5 tablespoons olive oil

Place the salmon steaks on small pieces of greased foil or baking parchment in a steamer. Place the potatoes in the steamer base and cover with boiling water. Add a little salt to the potatoes, if liked. Place the steamer on top and bring to the boil. Reduce the heat slightly and cook for 15 minutes, until the potatoes are tender and the salmon steaks are cooked.

Meanwhile, mix the lettuce, watercress, spinach, parsley, dill and chives in a large bowl. When well mixed, divide this salad between four serving bowls – large individual pasta bowls are ideal. Use the same large bowl to make the dressing: whisk the mustard, sugar, lemon zest and juice together with plenty of seasoning until the sugar and salt have dissolved. Then whisk in the olive oil.

Drain the potatoes and cut them in half or quarters, depending on how large they are, adding them to the dressing as they are cut. Turn the potatoes in the dressing to coat them evenly. Coarsely flake the salmon steaks and add to the potato salad, then mix very lightly. Pile the salmon and potato mixture on top of the salad and serve at once.

Prawn Wontons

Wonton wrappers are small squares of Chinese noodle dough (paste) used for making little dumplings and dim sum or snacks that can be boiled, steamed or fried. Wontons are often served in soup but they are also good with a dipping sauce. Serve these as a first course or with noodles or rice and stir-fried mixed vegetables for a light main course.

Serves 4

225 g/8 oz skinless, boneless white fish fillet

225 g/8 oz peeled cooked prawns (shrimp)

4 spring onions (scallions), finely chopped

2 tablespoons grated fresh ginger root

salt and pepper

1 small egg white

2 tablespoons cornflour (cornstarch)

about 36 wonton wrappers

a few Chinese leaves

Dipping Sauce

1 small garlic clove, thinly sliced

green part of 1 spring onion (scallion), finely chopped

6 tablespoons soy sauce

6 tablespoons dry sherry

½ teaspoon sesame oil

Purée the fish fillet and prawns until just smooth in a food processor. Mix with the spring onions and ginger, adding a little salt and pepper. Stir in the egg white and enough cornflour to bind the mixture into a firm consistency.

Line a large steamer – or two tiers of a smaller one – with Chinese leaves. Place a wonton wrapper on the palm of one hand, brush it with a little water, then mound a little of the fish mixture in the middle. Press the wrapper around the fish to make a neat bundle, then place this in the steamer. Continue filling the wonton wrappers in this way, making sure they do not quite touch each other in the steamer (or they will stick together during cooking).

Steam the wontons over boiling water for 10–15 minutes. Meanwhile, mix all the ingredients for the dipping sauce and divide this between four small dishes. Serve the wontons on a warm platter or straight from the steamers if you are using Chinese bamboo steamers. The wontons are dunked in the dipping sauce before they are eaten.

DELECTABLE BAKED SEAFOOD

Swordfish in Tomato and Olive Sauce with Gremolada

Cooked in a rich sauce of good ingredients, firm swordfish is topped with zingy gremolada – a mixture of garlic, lemon and parsley – to make a substantial and nutritious meal. Serve with pasta or rice and a hearty mixed side salad, lightly cooked spinach or broccoli.

Serves 4

2 tablespoons olive oil

1 bay leaf

1 large onion, chopped

1 garlic clove, crushed

1 celery stick (stalk), chopped

1 carrot, chopped

½ teaspoon dried oregano

salt and pepper

400 g/14 oz can chopped tomatoes

150 ml/¼ pint/⅔ cup red wine

50 g/2 oz/⅓ cup pitted black olives, sliced

4 (100 g/4 oz) portions swordfish

Gremolada

grated zest of 1 lemon

large handful of parsley sprigs, chopped

1 garlic clove, chopped

Set the oven at 180°C, 350°F, Gas 4. Heat the oil in a small saucepan and add the bay leaf, onion, garlic, celery, carrot and oregano. Sprinkle with a little seasoning, stir well and cover the pan. Cook for 15 minutes. Stir in the tomatoes and wine and cook for a further 5 minutes. Stir in the olives and remove from the heat.

Place the swordfish steaks in a casserole. Taste the sauce for seasoning and add more salt and pepper if necessary, then pour it over the swordfish. Cover tightly and bake for 30 minutes. Check halfway through cooking and turn or baste the swordfish if necessary.

Meanwhile, mix the lemon, parsley and garlic for the gremolada. Arrange the swordfish on warmed plates, spooning over all the sauce from the casserole. Sprinkle with gremolada and serve at once.

Baked Stuffed Squid in Tomato Sauce

A lively garlic, green pepper and wholemeal breadcrumb stuffing brings goodness and delicious flavour to tender baked squid. Serve with brown or red Camargue rice and a crunchy, nutritious side salad of spinach, watercress, celery and courgettes (zucchini).

Serves 4

1 tablespoon olive oil
1 small onion, finely chopped
1 green (bell) pepper, cored and de-seeded, finely chopped
3 garlic cloves, finely chopped
1 tablespoon fresh thyme leaves
grated zest of ½ lemon
50 g/2 oz/1 cup fresh wholemeal breadcrumbs
8 skinless cleaned squid pouches

Tomato Sauce

1 tablespoon olive oil
1 large onion, chopped
1 garlic clove, crushed
1 small carrot, chopped
2 celery sticks (stalks), chopped
salt and pepper
2 (400 g/14 oz) cans chopped tomatoes
½ teaspoon sugar
4 tablespoons dry sherry

Make the tomato sauce first. Place the oil in a saucepan and add the onion, garlic, carrot and celery. Season lightly, then cover and cook over medium heat for about 15 minutes, stirring occasionally, until the vegetables are softened slightly, but not browned. Stir in the tomatoes, sugar and sherry and bring to the boil. Reduce the heat and cover the pan, and then simmer the sauce for 15 minutes. Taste for seasoning.

Prepare the stuffing for the squid: place the olive oil, onion, green pepper, garlic and thyme in a small saucepan. Mix well, cover and cook over medium heat for 10 minutes. Remove the lid and cook, stirring, for a further 5 minutes, to evaporate any cooking juices from the vegetables. Remove from the heat and stir in the lemon zest. Cool slightly before stirring in the breadcrumbs with seasoning to taste.

Set the oven at 180°C, 350°F, Gas 4. Use a small teaspoon to put the stuffing into the squid, allowing space for the stuffing to swell during cooking. Pin a wooden cocktail stick across the top of each squid pouch to close the opening. Place the squid in an ovenproof casserole and ladle the sauce over. Cover and bake for 45 minutes, until the squid is tender and the stuffing well cooked.

Monkfish with Leeks and Parma Ham

Lightly cooked leeks and a sprinkling of Parma ham make a delicious topping for firm, fine-flavoured monkfish. Serve with potatoes and carrots, mashed together, and lightly cooked spinach. Anglerfish may be used instead.

Serves 4

2 tablespoons olive oil

1 leek, thinly sliced

salt and pepper

600 g/1 lb 5 oz prepared monkfish (anglerfish)

75 g/3 oz Parma ham, cut into fine shreds

50 g/2 oz/⅓ cup mozzarella cheese, finely diced

Set the oven at 180°C, 350°F, ©as 4. Heat the olive oil in a saucepan and add the leek with a little salt and pepper. Cook for 10 minutes, stirring occasionally, until the leek has softened and the liquid it yields has evaporated.

Cut the monkfish into eight neat portions and place them in a shallow ovenproof dish. Taste the leeks and add a little extra seasoning, if necessary, then spoon them over the fish. Sprinkle with the Parma ham, then add the mozzarella cheese. Bake for 30 minutes, until the topping is bubbling and lightly browned. Serve at once.

Trout with Mushroom and Ham Stuffing

A little cooked ham gives depth of flavour to mushroom stuffing, while plenty of parsley and lemon zest taste lively and fresh.

Serves 4

1 tablespoons olive oil
1 onion, finely chopped
salt and pepper
100 g/4 oz closed cap mushrooms, chopped
50 g/2 oz cooked ham, finely chopped
50 g/2 oz/1 cup fresh wholemeal breadcrumbs
grated zest of 1 lemon
handful of parsley sprigs, chopped
4 trout, cleaned with heads and tails on
lemon wedges and parsley sprigs to garnish

Heat the oil in a small saucepan. Add the onion with a little seasoning and cover the pan. Cook for 5 minutes. Add the mushrooms, stir well and cover the pan, then continue to cook for 15 minutes, stirring occasionally. Stir in the ham and cook, uncovered, for a few minutes to evaporate any excess liquor. Stir in the breadcrumbs, taste and add seasoning, if necessary.

Set the oven at 180°C, 350°F, Gas 4. Grease a shallow ovenproof dish. Divide the stuffing between the 4 trout, using a teaspoon to press it into their body cavities. Place in the dish and cover with foil, then bake for 35–40 minutes, until the fish are cooked. Serve the trout garnished with lemon wedges and parsley sprigs.

Serves 4

4 (175 g/6 oz) portions halibut steak
4 small thyme sprigs
salt and pepper
4 tablespoons shelled unsalted pistachio nuts, coarsely
chopped
4 spring onions (scallions), chopped
grated zest and juice of 1 orange
40 g/1½ oz/3 tablespoons butter
4 tablespoons reduced-fat crème fraîche

Set the oven at 180°C, 350°F, Gas 4. Place the portions of halibut steak on a shallow ovenproof dish. Pick the tiny leaves off the thyme sprigs and sprinkle them over the fish. Season the halibut and top with the nuts, spring onions and orange zest. Spoon the orange juice evenly over the top and dot with the butter.

Cover with foil and bake for 20–25 minutes, until the fish is just cooked. Turn the oven off. Stir the crème fraîche into the juices around the fish, cover and return to the oven for a further 5 minutes to heat the cream through. Serve freshly cooked.

Halibut Steaks with Pistachio and Orange

The light flavour and tender texture of pistachio nuts go well with fish. Serve a mixture of stir-fried green vegetables to complement this dish – try broccoli with shredded pak choy, adding some chopped watercress right at the end (after removing the pan from the heat) for a slightly peppery flavour.

Baked Sea Bass

Baking is a practical method when cooking one fish per portion, as steaming or pan-frying can present space problems. As well as being a popular fish in Chinese cooking – often steamed with ginger and other quite distinctive ingredients – sea bass tastes excellent with the minimum of additional flavouring.

Serves 4

4 (350 g/12 oz) sea bass, gutted with heads and tails on
3 tablespoons olive oil, plus extra for greasing
4 strips of pared lemon peel
8 bay leaves
salt and pepper
40 g/1½ oz/3 tablespoons butter
2 tablespoons lemon juice
2 tablespoons capers, chopped
4 tablespoons chopped parsley

Set the oven at 180°C, 350°F, Gas 4. Cut 4 double-thick sheets of foil, each large enough to enclose a fish. Grease the foil with a little olive oil.

Place a strip of lemon peel and 2 bay leaves in the body cavity of a fish and sprinkle with seasoning. Wrap in foil, folding the edges together to seal in all the juices, and place on a baking (cookie) sheet. Repeat with the remaining fish. Bake for 40 minutes, until the flesh of the fish is opaque and firm.

Heat the olive oil, butter, lemon juice and capers together gently until the butter has melted. Stir in the parsley and a little seasoning, then remove from the heat. Transfer the sea bass to warmed plates and spoon the flavoured butter and oil over it.

Mackerel with Fennel and Apple

Sweet-sour apples and slightly aniseed fennel are delicious with rich mackerel and they also contribute fruit and vegetable food value in the form of essential vitamins and important phytochemicals. Serve with crisp-baked salad potatoes or new potatoes and vegetables, such as broccoli and carrots.

Serves 4

3 tablespoons olive oil
1 large onion, halved and thinly sliced
2 fennel bulbs, halved and thinly sliced
salt and pepper
2 crisp, sharp-sweet dessert apples
juice of 1 lemon
2 tablespoons sugar
4 mackerel, gutted, with heads and tails removed

Set the oven at 190 °C, 375 °F, Gas 5. Heat 1 tablespoon of the oil in a small saucepan and add the onion and fennel. Season lightly, stir well and cover the pan. Cook gently for 20 minutes, until the vegetables are just tender, but not browned.

Meanwhile, peel, core and slice the apples into rings, placing them in the lemon juice in a bowl to prevent them from discolouring. Transfer the onion and fennel to a shallow ovenproof dish large enough to hold the mackerel. Trim any fins off the mackerel and place them one their sides on top of the onion and fennel. Season well.

Divide the apple slices between the mackerel, overlapping them neatly. Sprinkle with the lemon juice remaining in the bowl. Carefully sprinkle the sugar over the apple slices, then bake for 20–30 minutes, until the apples are browned and the mackerel are cooked.

Tuna with Tomatoes and Peppers

Tomatoes and (bell) peppers go well with all firm, slightly meaty fish: alternatives to tuna include swordfish or marlin. The vegetables keep the fish moist during cooking and create a well-balanced, full-flavoured dish. Serve rice or noodles and a good mixed green salad as accompaniments.

Serves 4

3 tablespoons olive oil
4 bay leaves
2 garlic cloves, crushed
2 red onions, halved and thinly sliced
2 red (bell) peppers, de-seeded, halved and thinly sliced
2 green (bell) peppers, de-seeded, halved and thinly sliced
salt and pepper
4 (100 g/4 oz) portions tuna steak
500 g/1 lb 2 oz ripe tomatoes, peeled and thinly sliced
100 g/4 oz/½ cup ricotta cheese
Parmesan cheese shavings to serve

Set the oven at 200°C, 400°F, Gas 6. Heat the oil in a frying pan (skillet) and add the bay leaves, garlic, onions, and red and green peppers. Season to taste and cook, stirring occasionally, for about 10 minutes, or until the vegetables are softened but not browned.

Spoon half the peppers and onions in an even layer in a shallow ovenproof dish. Add half the tomatoes and arrange the tuna portions on top. Spoon the remaining peppers over the tuna and top with the remaining tomatoes. Dot lumps of the ricotta cheese over the tomatoes and bake for 25–30 minutes, until the tuna is cooked and the cheese is browned in places. Serve at once, topping each portion with a few Parmesan cheese shavings.

Bubbling Salmon Fish Cakes

On its own, as here, or used half and half with white fish, fresh salmon makes delicious fish cakes. Baking is a healthier method than frying or sautéeing, and the topping of bubbling mozzarella cheese is delicious.

Serves 4

450 g/1 lb salmon fillet, skinned

700 g/1 lb 9 oz potatoes, boiled, mashed and cooled

4 tablespoons chopped parsley

4 tablespoons snipped chives

salt and pepper

about 6 tablespoons uncooked semolina

100 g/4 oz/½ cup mozzarella cheese, thinly sliced

oil for greasing

Set the oven at 200°C, 400°F, Gas 4. Remove any bones from the salmon, then finely chop it. Mix the chopped salmon into the mashed potatoes with the parsley and chives. Add seasoning and mix thoroughly.

Grease a large shallow baking dish with oil. Divide the mixture into eight portions. Sprinkle the semolina on a large plate. Use two dessert spoons to shape a portion of the fish mixture into a mound on the semolina. Flatten the mixture with the back of a spoon, then shape it into a neat round cake and coat with the semolina. Transfer to the greased dish and repeat with the remaining mixture.

Top the fish cakes with the mozzarella and sprinkle with a little extra semolina. Bake for about 30 minutes, until golden brown. Serve at once.

Fish Pie with Fabulous Green Mash

Instead of adding lots of butter, go for the vegetable goodness and fabulous flavour of spinach, broccoli and herbs in a mashed potato topping for this traditional fish pie.

Serves 4-6

500 g/1 lb 2 oz white fish fillet
600 ml/1 pint/2½ cups milk
1 small onion, finely chopped
2 celery sticks (stalks), finely chopped
2 carrots, chopped
salt and pepper
40 g/1½ oz/3 tablespoons butter
100 g/4 oz mushrooms, thinly sliced
40 g/1½ oz/1½ tablespoons plain (all-purpose) flour

Green Mash

1 kg/2 lb 4 oz potatoes
1 tablespoons olive oil
450 g/1 lb spinach, finely shredded
100 g/4 oz broccoli, chopped
bunch of chives, finely snipped
handful of parsley, chopped

Crispy Topping

25 g/1 oz/⅓ cup Cheddar cheese, finely grated
25 g/1 oz/½ cup fairly dry white breadcrumbs

Place the fish in a frying pan (skillet) or suitable saucepan and pour in the milk. Heat gently until simmering, then cook gently for about 5 minutes, until the fish is firm and just cooked. Drain the fish, reserving the milk. Discard the skin and bones, leaving the fish in large chunks.

Melt the butter in a saucepan and add the onion, celery and carrots. Season lightly, then cook for 15 minutes, stirring often, until the vegetables are softened but not browned. Stir in the mushrooms and cook for a further 5 minutes. Stir in the flour, then gradually pour in the milk used for cooking the fish. Bring to the boil, stirring continuously. Remove from the heat and taste for seasoning. Add the fish and pour the sauce into a large, deep ovenproof casserole or dish.

Cut the potatoes into small cubes and cook in boiling salted water for 10–15 minutes, until tender. Drain well, then mash thoroughly until smooth. Set the oven at 200°C, 400°F, Gas 6.

Place the olive oil in the saucepan and add the spinach. Cover the pan and cook over medium heat, shaking the pan often, for about 10 minutes, or until the spinach is well cooked. Use a draining spoon to remove the spinach from the pan and transfer it to a sieve. Firmly press out the liquid from the spinach, letting it drip back into the pan. Then add the spinach to the mashed potatoes.

Add the broccoli to the spinach liquid and cook, stirring, for 3–5 minutes, until the broccoli is tender and most of the liquid has evaporated. Add the broccoli, chives and parsley to the potatoes. Mix lightly and taste for seasoning.

Top the fish and sauce with the green mash, spreading it out evenly. Mark the top in fairly deep ridges with a fork. Mix the cheese and breadcrumbs, then sprinkle this evenly over the top of the pie. Bake for about 20 minutes or until the top of the pie is crisp and golden, and the sauce is bubbling hot. Serve at once.

Note: Suitable Fish The slightly softer white fish are ideal for making pie (rather than firm and meaty swordfish or marlin). While cod or haddock are the traditional British favourites, pollock, whiting, haddock, hoki, hake or coley are all suitable. Smoked fish, such as haddock or cod, are excellent, especially when used half and half with white fish. Salmon or tuna are also good. For a punchy pie, try mackerel, adding the grated zest of 1 lemon and 1–2 tablespoons creamed horseradish to the sauce to cut the rich flavour of the fish.

Swordfish with Walnut, Mushroom and Olive Crust

A crunchy crust seals in flavour and moisture when baking sturdy swordfish. Serve noodles dressed with herbs and a little olive oil or coarsely crushed potatoes moistened with a little Greek-style yogurt; green beans or peas will complete the meal.

Serves 4

3 tablespoons olive oil
2 garlic cloves, crushed
I small onion, finely chopped
225 g/8 oz mushrooms, chopped
salt and pepper
50 g/2 oz/⅔ cup pitted black olives, chopped
50 g/2 oz/½ cup walnuts, chopped
50 g/2 oz/I cup fresh wholemeal breadcrumbs
4 tablespoons chopped parsley
4 swordish steaks, about 150 g/5 oz each

Heat 2 tablespoons of the oil in a saucepan. Add the garlic and onion, and cook for 5 minutes, until the onion has softened slightly. Add the mushrooms with salt and pepper, then cook until all the liquor yielded by the mushrooms has evaporated. Stir frequently during this time. Stir in the olives and walnuts, then remove from the heat and leave to cool.

Set the oven at 190°C, 375°F, Gas 5. Mix the breadcrumbs and parsley into the walnut mixture and taste for seasoning. Place the swordfish steaks in a shallow ovenproof dish and divide the walnut mixture between them. Spread the mixture evenly over the steaks. Sprinkle the remaining oil over and bake for 25–30 minutes, or until the topping is browned and crusty.

Grilled Sardines with Piquant Lemon Salad

Sardines are bursting with flavour and all the goodness oily fish has to offer. They are delicious plainly grilled (broiled), with plenty of seasoning and several lemon wedges per portion for contrasting sharp flavour. This recipe takes the basic flavours a step further with a terrific salad – it is one of my favourite salads for serving with all sorts of rich main ingredients. Marinating finely chopped lemon with sugar, salt and garlic makes a delicious salsa-style dressing for leaves that is full of punchy flavours. For a satisfying main course, offer lots of warm crusty bread with the sardines; halve the quantities to make a generous appetizer.

Serves 4

16 sardines, cleaned with heads on

Piquant Lemon Salad

1 small thin-skinned lemon, scrubbed
1 garlic clove, finely chopped
6 spring onions (scallions), finely chopped
1 mild green chilli, de-seeded and finely chopped (optional)
1 green (bell) pepper, cored, de-seeded and finely diced
salt and pepper
2 tablespoons sugar
4 tablespoons olive oil
175 g/6 oz watercress
100 g/4 oz rocket
100 g/4 oz lamb's lettuce

Make the base for the lemon salad at least 1 hour in advance – it can be prepared several hours before the leaves are added. Discard the tips off the ends of the lemon, then cut it in half and pick out any pips. Chop the lemon – skin and all – discarding the pips as you come across them. Place the lemon in a large bowl with the garlic, spring onions, chilli (if using) and green pepper. Sprinkle with a little salt and pepper, and the sugar. Cover and leave to marinate.

The sardines cook quickly, so finish preparing the salad while preheating the grill (broiler) on the hottest setting. Stir the olive oil into the lemon mixture. Add the watercress, rocket and lamb's lettuce to the bowl but do not toss the leaves with the lemon yet.

Season the sardines with salt and pepper and cook them under the hot grill (broiler) for 3–5 minutes on each side. Transfer them to large, warmed plates. Toss the salad and add some to each plate, offering the rest separately. Serve at once, while still hot.

Crab Omelettes with Stir-fried Vegetables

Light omelettes made with egg whites make a delicious lunch or supper with stir-fried vegetables. For a more substantial meal, add cooked Chinese noodles to the stir-fried vegetables.

Serves 4

1 tablespoon cornflour (cornstarch)
4 tablespoons water
4 egg whites
a few drops of sesame oil
salt
4 spring onions (scallions), finely chopped
1 tablespoon finely grated fresh ginger root
200 g/7 oz white crab meat (drained canned, frozen or fresh)
sunflower oil for cooking

Stir-fried Vegetables

200 g/7 oz baby sweetcorn (baby corn)
200 g/7 oz mangetout (snow) peas
6 spring onions (scallions), sliced at an angle
2 heads of pak choi, shredded
1–2 tablespoons light soy sauce

Mix the cornflour to a smooth paste with the water in a bowl. Add the egg whites, sesame oil and a little salt and whisk until mixed and light but not too frothy. Whisk in the spring onions and ginger, then stir in the crab meat.

For the stir-fried vegetables, cook the sweetcorn in boiling water for 4 minutes. Add the mangetout, bring back to the boil and drain immediately. Add the spring onions to the sweetcorn mixture and set aside. Prepare a wok or large frying pan (skillet) for cooking the vegetables, adding the minimum of sunflower oil.

Heat another large non-stick frying pan (skillet) with the minimum of sunflower oil. Drop spoonfuls of the crab mixture into the pan and spread them out with the back of the spoon so that each is evenly thick. Cook until set and golden underneath, then turn and cook the second side. Transfer to a warmed plate and keep hot while cooking the rest of the mixture to make eight small crab omelettes.

While the second batch of omelettes is cooking, heat the pan for the vegetables, then stir-fry the sweetcorn mixture for 1–2 minutes. Add the pak choy and cook for a further 1–2 minutes, until it has just wilted. Stir in soy sauce to taste and divide between four warmed plates. Arrange the crab omelettes on the plates and serve at once.

Grilled Mackerel with Gooseberry Sauce

Sharp and fruity gooseberries are a classic accompaniment for rich mackerel, either in a stuffing or served as a sauce. This recipe also works well with herring.

Serves 4

4 mackerel (herring), cleaned with heads off
salt and pepper
a little olive oil

Gooseberry Sauce
75 g/3 oz/⅓ cup sugar
2 tablespoons water
225 g/8 oz gooseberries, topped and tailed

First make the gooseberry sauce: place the sugar in a saucepan and add the water. Heat gently, stirring, until the sugar has dissolved, then bring to the boil. Stir in the gooseberries and reduce the heat so that the fruit simmers gently. Cook for 10–15 minutes, until the gooseberries are soft. Set aside off the heat.

Trim any fins off the mackerel and place them on their side on the rack in a grill (broiler) pan. Season well and drizzle with a hint of olive oil, then grill (broil) for 3–5 minutes, until browned and crisp. Use a fish slice and fork to turn the fish, taking care not to break them. Season and moisten with olive oil, then cook for a further 3–5 minutes, until both sides are lightly browned.

Transfer the mackerel to warmed plates. Add a little gooseberry sauce to each plate and serve the rest separately.

Marinated Squid with Garlic and Chilli

Serve stir-fried mixed vegetables, such as spring onions (scallions), beansprouts and shredded Chinese leaves, with these spicy squid skewers. Add rice or noodles for a hearty main course.

Serves 4

1 green chilli, de-seeded and chopped
3 garlic cloves, chopped
1 spring onion (scallion), chopped
3 tablespoons sunflower oil
4 tablespoons light soy sauce
2 teaspoons sugar
3 tablespoons lemon juice
4 tablespoons dry sherry
16 clean white squid sacs

Purée the chilli, garlic, spring onion, sunflower oil, soy sauce, sugar, lemon juice and sherry until smooth in a blender or food processor. Pour into a bowl or small casserole.

Cut the squid sacs in half lengthwise, down each side. Use a small, very sharp knife to score a diamond pattern on the inside surface of each piece of squid, taking care to avoid cutting right through the flesh. Add the squid to the pureed marinade as it is prepared. Use a spoon to mix the squid with the sauce, ensuring all the pieces are well coated. Cover and leave to marinate for several hours.

Preheat the grill (broiler) on the hottest setting. Thread the pieces of squid on to four long or eight short metal skewers, draining each piece well. Transfer the marinade to a small saucepan and bring to a full boil, stirring. Divide the boiled marinade between four small dishes.

Cook the squid close to the heat source for 3–4 minutes on each side, until curled and well browned in places. Serve at once, offering the marinade as a dipping sauce.

Grilled Hake with Parsley and Almond Sauce

A cold sauce of almonds puréed with parsley, lemon and olive oil makes a delicious and healthy dressing for grilled hake. Couscous, rice or potatoes will complement the flavours of the fish and sauce.

Serves 4

4 portions hake fillet, about 175 g/6 oz each

Parsley and Almond Sauce
50 g/2 oz parsley sprigs
50 g/2 oz/⅓ cup blanched almonds
grated zest of 1 lemon
1 tablespoon lemon juice
100 ml/4½ fl oz/⅓ cup olive oil plus a little extra
salt and pepper

Make the sauce before cooking the fish. Process the parsley and almonds in a food processor or blender until finely chopped. Add the lemon zest and juice, then process again, gradually adding the olive oil to make a smooth paste. Taste and add a little seasoning.

Preheat the grill (broiler) on the hottest setting. Place the hake in a shallow flameproof dish and brush with a little olive oil. Season lightly and grill (broil) for 3–4 minutes, then turn the fish and cook the second side for 3–4 minutes or until the fish is opaque and flakes easily. Transfer to warmed plates and top with a little of the sauce. Offer the remaining sauce separately.

Swordfish with Avocado and Lime Salsa

This juicy salsa spiked with chilli and refreshed by diced cucumber tastes terrific with grilled swordfish. Serve with plenty of colourful rice, tossed with freshly cooked peas and halved cherry tomatoes.

Serves 4

2 tablespoons chopped fresh marjoram
4 tablespoons olive oil
grated zest and juice of 1 lime
salt and pepper
4 portions swordfish, about 175 g/6 oz each
1 green chilli, de-seeded and chopped
1 garlic clove, finely chopped

½ cucumber, finely diced
4 spring onions (scallions), finely chopped
2 avocados, halved, stoned (pitted), peeled and finely chopped
4 tablespoons chopped fresh coriander (cilantro)

Place the portions of swordfish in a shallow flameproof dish and sprinkle with the marjoram. Pour over 1 tablespoon of the olive oil and the juice of ½ lime. Season well, cover and set aside to marinate for 1–2 hours.

Meanwhile, mix the remaining olive oil and lime juice in a bowl. Add the chilli, garlic, cucumber, spring onions, avocados and coriander. Season and mix well, then cover closely with cling film (saran wrap), pressing it over the surface of the salsa. Set aside to marinate.

Preheat the grill (broiler) on a medium setting. Turn the pieces of swordfish over a couple of times in the dish so that both sides are coated with the oil and lime juice. Grill (broil) for 5–8 minutes on each side, until the fish is opaque and flakes easily. Transfer to warmed plates and top with a little salsa. Serve at once, offering the remaining salsa separately.

Pan-fried Plaice with Mushrooms in Vermouth

A little vermouth, crème fraîche and dill (dill weed) suddenly transform a pan of sautéed mushrooms into a luxurious sauce for delicate plaice fillets. This recipe works well with most white fish fillets or steaks (adjust the cooking time according to their thickness) and with salmon.

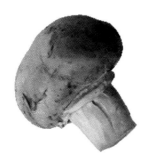

Serves 4

4 light-skinned plaice (flounder/sole) fillets
salt and pepper
plain (all-purpose) flour for coating
25 g/1 oz/2 tablespoons butter
3 tablespoons sunflower oil
100 g/4 oz button mushrooms, sliced
4 tablespoons dry white vermouth
150 ml/¼ pint/⅔ cup crème fraîche
2 tablespoons snipped chives
2 tablespoons chopped dill (dill weed)

Pat the plaice fillets dry with paper towels. Season well and dust lightly with a little flour. Heat half the butter and half the sunflower oil together in a large frying pan (skillet), then add 2 plaice fillets, skin sides up.

Cook for 2 minutes, then use a fish slice to turn the fillets and cook for a further 2 minutes or until the fish is lightly browned on both sides. Transfer the fish fillets to warmed plates and keep hot while cooking the remaining fish in the remaining oil and butter.

Transfer the last of the cooked fish fillets to the warmed plates. Add the mushrooms to the fat remaining in the pan and cook over high heat, stirring. Pour in the vermouth, add seasoning and bring to the boil. Boil rapidly for about 30 seconds, then remove from the heat. Stir in the crème fraîche and herbs.

Taste for seasoning and warm through for a few seconds if necessary – but do not overheat or the sauce will curdle. Spoon the mushroom sauce over the fish fillets and serve.

Scallops on Creamed Spinach

Scallops are expensive, and delicious – especially when plainly cooked and served with spinach enriched with just a touch of cream and perked up with a little nutmeg. Serve as a first course with warm wholemeal bread rolls or with rice as a main course.

Serves 4

3 tablespoons olive oil
1 kg/2¼ lb spinach, washed and shredded
salt and pepper
a little freshly grated nutmeg
20 scallops, cleaned
100 ml/4 fl oz/½ cup single (light) cream
2 tablespoons snipped chives
4 lemon wedges

Place 1 tablespoon of the olive oil in a large saucepan. Add the spinach, still slightly wet from washing, and seasoning. Cook over high heat for about 2 minutes, stirring the spinach as soon as it begins to wilt and reduce in volume. Cook for a few minutes longer, until the spinach is greatly reduced the liquor it yields has evaporated. Leave over low heat.

Heat the remaining oil in a non-stick frying pan (skillet). Add the scallops and cook over fairly high heat for about 1 minute on each side, or until just firm and browned. Take care not to overcook the scallops or they will shrink and become tough.

Pour the cream over the spinach, check the seasoning and heat gently for a few seconds. Divide the spinach between four warmed plates. Slice the scallops in half horizontally and place on top of the spinach. Sprinkle with chives and add a lemon wedge to each portion. Serve at once.

Stir-fried Tiger Prawns with Shittake Mushrooms

Prepare boiled rice or egg noodles as a base for this delicious stir fry. Raw tiger prawns (jumbo shrimp) are readily available frozen when they are not displayed among the selection of fresh fish.

Serves 4

2 tablespoons sunflower oil

coarsely grated zest from 1 lime

1 tablespoon finely chopped fresh ginger root

1 garlic clove, crushed

2 carrots, cut into short fine strips

1 bunch of spring onions (scallions), finely shredded

225 g/8 oz fresh shittake mushrooms, sliced

450 g/1 lb peeled raw tiger prawns (jumbo shrimp)

1 teaspoon cornflour (cornstarch)

6 tablespoons dry sherry

4 tablespoons light soy sauce

2 tablespoons chopped fresh coriander (cilantro)

Heat the oil in a large frying pan (skillet) or wok. Add the lime zest, ginger, garlic, carrots and spring onions. Stir-fry for 2 minutes, then add the mushrooms and prawns and continue to stir-fry for 2–3 minutes.

Mix the cornflour to a paste with the sherry and soy sauce, then pour this into the pan and bring to the boil, stirring. Cook gently for 1 minute or until all the prawns are pink and tender. Do not overcook the prawns or they will shrink and toughen. Sprinkle with chopped coriander and serve at once.

Salmon, Fennel and Broccoli Sauce

Fennel and broccoli are brimming with the naturally good ingredients found in plants to complement the benefits of oily fish in a healthy diet. The vegetables taste terrific with the salmon and the sauce goes well with pasta, rice or couscous.

Serves 4

750 g/1½ lb salmon fillet
3 bay leaves
300 ml/½ pint/1¼ cups water
300 ml/½ pint dry white wine
450 g/1 lb broccoli, cut into small florets
2 tablespoons olive oil
1 onion, finely chopped
1 fennel bulb, chopped
salt and pepper
3 tablespoons plain (all-purpose) flour
200 ml/7 fl oz/1 cup Greek-style yogurt
handful of parsley, chopped

Place the salmon in a large saucepan. Crumple the bay leaves to help release their flavour and add them to the salmon, then pour in the water and wine. Heat gently until just simmering. Poach the salmon for about 3 minutes, until it is just firm but not quite cooked through. Use a draining spoon or fish slice to drain the salmon. Flake the flesh in chunks off the skin, discarding the skin and any bones, then set the salmon aside.

Add the broccoli to the poaching liquor from the fish and bring to the boil. Boil, uncovered, for 3–4 minutes, until the broccoli is just tender. Drain the broccoli in a sieve over a bowl to reserve the cooking liquid and set both aside.

Rinse and dry the pan, then cook the olive oil, onion, fennel and seasoning to taste over moderate heat, stirring for about 1 minute or until the vegetables are beginning to sizzle. Cover the pan and cook gently for 15 minutes, until the vegetables are tender.

Stir the flour into the vegetables, then pour in the reserved cooking liquid and bring to the boil, stirring continuously. Reduce the heat and simmer the sauce gently for 5 minutes. Taste for seasoning, then add the broccoli and cook for a minute before adding the salmon. Cook gently for 1–2 minutes until the salmon is hot and completely cooked. Remove the pan from the heat and stir in the yogurt. Taste the sauce again for seasoning before adding the parsley and serving.

Quick Tuna Sauce

Canned tuna is one of the must-have storecupboard ingredients for whizzing up tasty and healthy supper dishes. Keep a good supply of frozen vegetables handy too – peas, sweetcorn (corn), spinach, green beans and broccoli florets are all good frozen, both for flavour and food value. Finally, remember to stock up on frozen herbs – the inexpensive way is to grow plenty in summer and freeze them chopped and ready for instant flavour. If your bay tree is not big enough to satisfy your culinary needs but you know someone with a large mature specimen, freeze whole fresh bay leaves as they keep for years to give far better flavour than dried leaves. For a low-fat version use tuna canned in brine or water and use 2 tablespoons olive oil for cooking the onion. Serve the sauce with rice, pasta or couscous, or ladled into baked potatoes.

Serves 4

200 g/7 oz can tuna in olive or sunflower oil
1 large onion, chopped
1 large carrot, diced
100 g/4 oz button mushrooms, roughly chopped
1 bay leaf
salt and pepper
40 g/1½ oz/2½ tablepoons plain (all-purpose) flour
600 ml/1 pint/2½ cups emi-skimmed milk
225 g/8 oz frozen sweetcorn (corn)
100 g/8 oz frozen petits pois
4 tablespoons chopped parsley

Drain the oil from the tuna into a saucepan. Add the onion, carrot, mushrooms, bay leaf and a little seasoning. Heat gently, stirring, until the vegetables begin to sizzle, then cover the pan and cook for 15 minutes or until the vegetables are tender.

Stir in the flour, then gradually pour in the milk and bring to the boil, stirring continuously. Add the sweetcorn and petits pois. Bring back to simmering point, cover and cook gently for 5 minutes. Flake the tuna into the sauce, mix lightly and taste for seasoning. Add the chopped parsley and serve at once.

Serves 4

2 tablespoons olive oil
1 large onion, chopped
2 garlic cloves, finely chopped
1 teaspoon dried marjoram
pinch of dried red chilli flakes (to taste)
1 red (bell) pepper, cored, de-seeded and diced
2 celery sticks (stalks), thinly sliced
2 carrots, diced
100 g/4 oz mushrooms, roughly chopped
salt and pepper
2 (400 g/14 oz) cans chopped tomatoes
100 ml/4 fl oz/¼ cup dry sherry, wine (red or white) or cider
225 g/8 oz cut green beans, frozen or fresh
450 g/1 lb frozen peeled cooked prawns (shrimp)
handful of parsley, chopped
grated zest of 1 lemon

Piquant Prawn and Tomato Sauce

This is another of those recipes for transforming a few stand-by ingredients into an impressively healthy mid-week meal, especially when you throw together a leafy salad accompaniment and round the meal off with fresh fruit. Ladle the sauce over spaghetti, rice, couscous or polenta.

Heat the oil in a large saucepan for a few seconds. Add the onion, half the garlic, marjoram, chilli flakes, red pepper, celery, carrots, mushrooms and a good sprinkling of seasoning. Stir well, cover the pan and cook over moderate heat for about 15 minutes, stirring occasionally, until the vegetables are quite tender.

Stir in the tomatoes and sherry, wine or cider and bring to the boil. Simmer for 2 minutes. Add the beans, bring back to the boil, reduce the heat and cover the pan. Cook for 5 minutes or until the beans are tender.

Add the frozen prawns and cook gently for about 2 minutes, stirring often, until they have thawed and reheated. Taste for seasoning and serve topped with the remaining garlic mixed with the parsley and lemon zest.

Fabulous Seafood Sauce

This versatile sauce will see you through many
an unobtrusively healthy and perfectly
indulgent menu. The sauce may be served
simply, with freshly cooked noodles or rice
tossed with a little grated lemon zest and
chopped watercress, or used in any of the
many ways suggested at the end of the recipe.

Serves 4

3 tablespoons olive oil

I small onion, finely chopped

I celery stick (stalk), finely diced

I carrot, finely diced

I bay leaf

I blade of mace

pared strip of lemon rind

4 tablespoons chopped parsley

100 g/4 oz baby button mushrooms

salt and pepper

40 g/1½ oz/2½ tablespoons plain (all-purpose) flour

600 ml/1 pint dry white wine

225 g/8 oz peeled raw tiger prawns (jumbo shrimp)

450 g/1 lb salmon fillet or steak, skinned, boned and cut into

chunks

8 scallops, cleaned and sliced

225 g/8 oz shelled cooked mussels

150 ml/¼ pint/⅔ cup Greek-style yogurt

4 tablespoons chopped dill (dill weed)

Heat the olive oil in a large saucepan. Add the onion, celery, carrot, bay leaf, blade of mace, strip of lemon rind, parsley, mushrooms and a little seasoning. Cook for 2 minutes, stirring, until the vegetables begin to sizzle, then reduce the heat and cover the pan. Cook for about 15 minutes, stirring occasionally, until the vegetables are tender and juicy.

Stir the flour into the vegetables, then gradually pour in the wine, stirring continuously, and bring to the boil. Reduce the heat, cover the pan and cook the sauce very gently for 15 minutes.

Bring the sauce back to a steady simmer and stir in the prawns, then add the salmon, cover and reduce the heat, if necessary, so that the sauce just simmers.

Cook gently for 5–7 minutes, until the prawns are pink and the salmon just cooked. Add the scallops, cover the pan again and simmer for about 2 minutes.

Finally, stir in the mussels with seasoning to taste and heat gently without boiling. When all the seafood is cooked and hot, remove the pan from the heat and stir in the yogurt and dill. Serve at once.

Ways to Serve Seafood Sauce

- Ladle over freshly cooked pasta shells or noodles, rice or mashed potatoes.

- Pipe creamy mashed potato to border large shell-shaped ovenproof dishes and heat gently in the oven. Spoon the sauce into the middle and serve. Alternatively, add the uncooked fish as for the pie below, and bake the sauce and potatoes together until cooked and lightly browned.

- Use the sauce as a filling for fabulous fish pie, topped with creamy mashed potatoes. When the sauce is cooked in the oven for this or the lasagne, below, remove the pan from the heat before adding the seafood, salmon, yogurt and dill (dill weed). Then allow these raw ingredients to cook during the baking time otherwise they will be overcooked in the finished dish.

- Layer the sauce with sheets of cooked fresh lasagne and top with a Béchamel sauce, then bake for about 30 minutes at 180°C, 350°F, Gas 4, or until golden.

- Use the sauce as a filling for pancakes. Coat with Béchamel sauce and brown in the oven, as for the lasagne above.

Cool Tuna and Watercress Sauce

With half fromage frais and home-made mayonnaise, this sauce is a healthy alternative to the usual tuna in mayonnaise. Bought mayonnaise can be used instead but select a high-quality product, for example one made with olive oil. The sauce can be served in a number of ways – one of the most popular is as a filling for large, fluffy baked potatoes. Pile the sauce into halved avocados or use it to fill warmed pitta bread or crusty baguettes; alternatively, toss it with freshly cooked pasta.

Serves 4

200 g/7 oz fresh tuna or 200 g/7 oz can tuna in brine, drained
1 egg yolk
pinch of caster sugar
salt and pepper
½ teaspoon Dijon mustard
juice of ½ lemon
100 ml/4 fl oz olive oil
200 ml/7 fl oz/1 cup low-fat fromage frais
100 g/4 oz watercress, chopped
4 spring onions (scallions), finely chopped
grated zest of ½ lemon
2 tablespoons chopped gherkins (cornichons)

If using fresh tuna, brush it with a little oil and grill (broil) it for about 15 minutes, turning once, or until the fish flakes easily. Place in a small bowl, cover and leave to cool completely.

Make a mayonnaise base for the sauce: place the egg yolk in a small bowl and whisk in the sugar, a little salt and pepper, the mustard and about half the lemon juice. Use a balloon whisk or single electric beater for this. Gradually add the olive oil in a very slow trickle at first, whisking hard to incorporate it with the egg mixture. It is best to add it drop by drop than to add too much, which will make the sauce curdle. Once the mixture begins to turn pale and thicken slightly, the oil can be added slightly faster. When the mayonnaise is thick, stir in the remaining lemon juice.

Flake the tuna finely in a bowl, then mix in the mayonnaise and gently stir in the fromage frais. Fold in the chopped watercress, spring onions (scallions), lemon zest and gherkin. Taste for seasoning and serve.

<u>Serves 4</u>

2 tablespoons tomato purée (paste)

2 teaspoons sugar

½ teaspoon paprika

1 tablespoon balsamic vinegar

2 tablespoons olive oil

450 g/1 lb ripe tomatoes, peeled, de-seeded and chopped

1 small red onion, finely chopped

1 red (bell) pepper, core discarded and finely chopped

2 garlic cloves, finely chopped

1 red chilli, finely chopped, or generous pinch of dried red chilli flakes

1 teaspoon dried oregano

salt and pepper

Mix the tomato purée, sugar, paprika and balsamic vinegar in a bowl. Stir well until the ingredients are thoroughly combined, then stir in the olive oil. Stir in all the remaining ingredients, cover and leave to marinate for several hours before serving.

Spicy Tomato Salsa

Combining fresh tomatoes with concentrated tomato purée (paste) ensures that this punchy salsa is absolutely bursting with flavour. Serve it with grilled, well-flavoured fish, such as tuna, swordfish, marlin, hoki, hake, salmon or mackerel.

Zesty Green Salsa

Serves 4

This lively mixture of (bell) peppers, rocket and coriander (cilantro) is good with pan-fried or grilled (broiled) fish. A mild green chilli gives the mixture a delicious hint of heat or use a small fiery chilli for a stronger result; if chilli is not your spice, the salsa has ample zest without it.

2 green (bell) peppers, core discarded and finely chopped

1 bunch of spring onions (scallions), finely chopped

1 green chilli, de-seeded and finely chopped

1 garlic clove, finely chopped

2 tablespoons capers, chopped

1 teaspoon sugar

salt and pepper

grated zest and juice of 1 lime

4 tablespoons olive oil

100 g/4 oz rocket, finely shredded

50 g/2 oz fresh coriander (cilantro) leaves, chopped

Mix the peppers, onions, chilli, garlic, capers, sugar and plenty of seasoning. Stir in the lime zest and juice followed by the olive oil. Leave this mixture to marinate for several hours or overnight. Stir in the rocket and coriander just before serving.

Light and Fresh Tomato and Basil Sauce

This light sauce is ideal as an accompaniment for fish or as a base in which to poach fish and seafood. Chunks of salmon, swordfish, monkfish, cod or peeled raw prawns (shrimp) can be cooked gently in the sauce and then served on pasta or rice.

Serves 4

2 tablespoons olive oil
1 large onion, finely chopped
1 celery stick (stalk), finely chopped
1 garlic clove, crushed
1 bay leaf
salt and pepper
1 kg/2¼ lb fresh ripe tomatoes, peeled, de-seeded and chopped
1 tablespoon tomato purée (paste)
1 teaspoon sugar
handful of tender basil sprigs

Heat the olive oil in a saucepan and add the onion, celery, garlic and bay leaf. Season lightly, then cook until the vegetables begin to sizzle. Stir well, cover and cook gently for about 20 minutes or until the vegetables are softened.

Stir in the tomatoes, tomato purée and sugar. Bring to the boil, then reduce the heat and cover the pan. Simmer for 20 minutes. Taste the sauce and add seasoning, with a little extra sugar, if necessary, to bring out the flavour of the tomatoes. Remove the pan from the heat and use kitchen scissors to shred the basil finely straight into the sauce just before serving.

Spinach Sauce

This is delicious with poached or steamed fish as well as with slightly richer grilled (broiled) or pan-fried fish and seafood.

Serves 4

2 tablespoons olive oil
1 small onion, finely chopped
1 bay leaf
1 blade of mace
2 tablespoons plain (all-purpose) flour
300 ml/½ pint/1¼ cup semi-skimmed milk
225 g/8 oz spinach, finely chopped
salt and pepper

Creamy Spinach Sauce

For a richer sauce, use full-cream milk and add 4–6 tablespoons single (light) cream or crème fraîche once the spinach has wilted.

Place the olive oil in a saucepan and add the onion, bay leaf and mace. Cover and cook very gently for 15 minutes, or until the onion has softened and the bay leaf and mace are aromatic.

Stir in the flour, then gradually add the milk, stirring continuously, and bring to the boil. Reduce the heat and cover the pan, then simmer the sauce gently for 5 minutes, stirring occasionally.

Add the spinach and cook, stirring, for 5 minutes, until the spinach has wilted completely into the sauce. Discard the bay leaf and blade of mace, then add seasoning to taste. The sauce is now ready to serve; however, for a completely smooth version, it can be puréed in a blender or pressed through a sieve.

Hot Salmon Salad with Red Leaves and Grapes

Freshly pan-fried salmon is one of my favourite ingredients for making brilliant hot salads. Tossing the freshly cooked fish with an excellent mix of leaves and punchy raw ingredients is one of the most stylish and delicious ways of serving it. Offer warmed, substantial and crusty, country-style French bread to accompany this salad for a satisfying lunch or supper.

Serves 4

450 g/1 lb salmon fillet, skinned and cut into
1.5 cm/¾ in chunks
4 tablespoons snipped chives
2 tablespoons chopped mint
juice of 1 lime or lemon
1 teaspoon sugar
1 tablespoon olive oil
1 lollo rosso, coarsely shredded
1 head of radicchio, shredded
½ small red onion, finely chopped
1 red (bell) pepper, cored, de-seeded and finely diced
175 g/6 oz seedless red grapes, halved
1 tablespoon sunflower oil
salt and pepper

Place the salmon in a bowl and sprinkle with the chives, mint, lime or lemon juice, sugar and olive oil. Cover and leave to marinate for 30 minutes.

Meanwhile, divide the lollo rosso, radicchio, onion, pepper and grapes evenly between four plates or bowls. Drain the salmon in a sieve over a bowl, reserving the marinade. Heat the sunflower oil in a non-stick frying pan (skillet). Season the salmon chunks and add them to the pan. Cook for about 2 minutes, until browned underneath, then turn or rearrange the pieces and cook for a further 2–3 minutes. The salmon should be firm, cooked and well browned in places.

Pour the reserved marinade over the salmon and swirl the pan to coat the pieces evenly. When the sizzling stops, spoon the salmon on to the salads, trickling the juices over the top. Serve immediately.

Mackerel on Greek Salad

Piquant mackerel with a dressing of capers, garlic and a hint of chilli is delicious on a salad of cucumber, (bell) pepper, tomato, onion, olives and feta cheese. This winning combination provides the mix of healthy ingredients for which Mediterranean meals are favoured.

Serves 4

4 mackerel, cleaned and boned
about 6 tablespoons plain (all-purpose) flour
salt and pepper
3 tablespoons olive oil
4 garlic cloves, thinly sliced
3 tablespoons capers, chopped
1 mild green chilli, de-seeded and chopped

Greek Salad

1 mild salad onion, halved and thinly sliced
½ cucumber, halved and thinly sliced
1 large green (bell) pepper, cored, de-seeded, quartered lengthwise and thinly sliced into short strips
50 g/2 oz/⅔ cup pitted black olives, thinly sliced
8 ripe tomatoes, de-seeded and cut into strips
100 g/4 oz feta/1 cup cheese, finely crumbled
2 lettuce hearts, shredded
8 lemon wedges to serve

Prepare the salad before cooking the mackerel. Mix the onion, cucumber, pepper, olives, tomatoes and feta cheese. Divide the lettuce hearts between four plates or wide bowls and top with the mixed salad. Set aside.

Check the opened-out mackerel for any bones, then dust with flour and season well. Heat 1 tablespoon of the oil in a large non-stick frying pan (skillet) and add two mackerel, skin sides up. Cook for 2–3 minutes until well browned, then use a fish slice to turn the mackerel and cook until well browned underneath. Transfer to a large plate and keep hot. Wipe the pan if there is any residue of browned flour before adding another tablespoon of oil and cooking the second batch of mackerel.

Wipe out the pan once more, then add the remaining oil, garlic, capers and chilli. Stir-fry for a few seconds, then remove from the heat and set aside. Cut the cooked mackerel across into strips and lay these in a criss-cross arrangement on top of the salad. Sprinkle the garlic, capers and chilli over the top and add a couple of lemon wedges to each salad. Serve at once.

Smoked Mackerel and Potato Salad

Blanched sugarsnap peas, beans and mixed salad leaves make an excellent base for the simple potato and mackerel mixture. Serve chunks of wholemeal bread to complete the meal.

Serves 4

700 g/1 lb 9 oz small new potatoes or salad potatoes
225 g/8 oz fine green beans
225 g/8 oz sugarsnap peas, sliced diagonally
200 g/7 oz mixed salad leaves, such as rocket, watercress, lamb's lettuce and baby spinach
4 spring onions (scallions), sliced
4 smoked mackerel fillets, skinned, boned and flaked

Dressing

1 tablespoon wholegrain mustard
2 tablespoons creamed horseradish
½ teaspoon sugar
salt and pepper
1 tablespoon cider vinegar
3 tablespoons olive oil

Cook the potatoes in boiling water for 15–20 minutes, until tender. Meanwhile, make the dressing: whisk the mustard, horseradish, sugar, seasoning and cider vinegar together in a bowl large enough to hold the potatoes and mackerel. Gradually whisk in the olive oil. Drain the cooked potatoes and add them to the dressing. Mix well, cover with a clean tea-towel or paper towels and leave to cool.

Bring a small saucepan of water to the boil, add the green beans and bring back to the boil. Boil for 1 minute, then add the sugarsnap peas and bring back to the boil. Drain immediately, refresh under cold water and drain well.

Divide the salad leaves between four bowls or place them in one large serving dish. Top with the beans and suparsnap peas. Add the spring onions and flaked mackerel to the potato salad and mix lightly. Pile the potato and mackerel salad on the vegetables and serve.

Smoked Salmon, Asparagus and Pasta Salad

Asparagus and smoked salmon are a summery combination with pasta shells in this luxurious salad. A variety of fish and seafood can be used instead of smoked salmon – for example, try poached monkfish or hake, peeled cooked prawns (shrimp) or sliced poached scallops; for a mixed seafood salad use a combination of white fish, prawns (shrimp) and scallops. Instead of serving the white fish, scallops or prawns on top of the asparagus, toss them with the pasta. Serve rye bread and butter to complement the salad.

Serves 4

225 g/8 oz pasta shells
salt and pepper
100 ml/4 fl oz/⅓ cup mayonnaise
200 ml/7 fl oz/⅔ cupow-fat fromage frais
4 tablespoons snipped chives
4 tablespoons chopped parsley
4 tablespoons chopped dill (dill weed)
salt and pepper
450 g/1 lb asparagus, trimmed
450 g/1 lb cherry tomatoes, halved
225 g/8 oz smoked salmon, cut into fine strips
1 lemon, cut into wedges

Cook the pasta shells in boiling salted water for 10–15 minutes, according to the instructions on the packet. Meanwhile, mix the mayonnaise and fromage frais in a large bowl. Stir in the chives, parsley, dill and seasoning. Drain the cooked pasta thoroughly, then rinse it under cold water and drain well. Toss the pasta with the herb dressing.

Cook the asparagus in simmering water for about 15 minutes, or until tender. (A tall asparagus cooker is ideal for this, allowing the tougher ends of the stalks to be cooked in the boiling water while the tender tips remain above the water to cook more gently in the steam.) Drain and leave until just cool.

Add the cherry tomatoes to the pasta salad, mixing them in very lightly. Do not overmix the salad as this will break up the tomatoes. Divide the pasta mixture between four plates or bowls, or place in one large serving dish. Top with the asparagus and then add the smoked salmon. Add lemon wedges and serve at once.

Tuna and Cannellini Bean Salad

This classic combination of ingredients is excellent for lunch or supper with plenty of crusty bread to mop up the delicious juices. Served in smaller portions it makes a tempting starter.

Serves 2 as a main course,

or 4 as a starter

1 tablespoon balsamic vinegar
pinch of salt
pinch of sugar
½ teaspoon wholegrain mustard
3 tablespoons olive oil
1 garlic clove, finely chopped
400 g/14 oz can cannellini beans, drained
1 mild red onion, thinly sliced
200 g/7 oz can tuna in brine or water, drained
handful of parsley, chopped

In a salad bowl, whisk the vinegar, salt, sugar and mustard together until the salt and sugar have dissolved. Whisk in the olive oil and garlic.

Add the cannellini beans and onion to the dressing. Turn these ingredients lightly to coat them evenly. Flake the tuna into the salad and mix lightly. Cover and leave to marinate for 1–2 hours if possible. Lightly mix in the parsley just before serving.

Serves 4

350 g/12 oz couscous
grated zest and juice of 1 lime
salt and pepper
1 teaspoon sugar
2 garlic cloves, finely chopped
4 tablespoons olive oil
450 g/1 lb tomatoes, peeled and chopped
8–10 spring onions (scallions), chopped
2 green (bell) peppers, cored de-seeded and finely diced
bunch of fresh coriander (cilantro) leaves, chopped
400 g/14 oz peeled cooked prawns (shrimp)

Place the couscous in a fairly small, deep bowl and pour in enough freshly boiling water to cover it by about 1 cm /½ in. Cover the bowl with cling film (saran wrap) and leave the couscous to soak for 15 minutes, or until the water has been absorbed and the couscous is plumped up and tender.

Prawn Couscous Salad

Couscous makes a great salad base for finely cut ingredients and its light texture is especially good with fish and seafood. Green (bell) pepper, tomato, spring onions, garlic, lime and coriander (cilantro) bring a punchy mix of flavours and lots of valuable vegetable nutrients to the salad. Serve with warmed, soft tortillas for scooping up the mixture.

Meanwhile, in a salad bowl, whisk the lime zest and juice with plenty of seasoning and the sugar until the sugar has dissolved. Whisk in the garlic and olive oil. Stir in the tomatoes, spring onions, peppers and coriander. Use a fork to fluff up the couscous and add it to the salad. Mix lightly, then add the prawns and continue mixing lightly until thoroughly combined. Leave salad to marinate for 1 hour before serving.

Crab and Egg Salad with Watercress Dressing

This is a good recipe for stretching one dressed crab to provide two portions at the same time as making a healthy main course. Serve wholemeal bread and butter, and boiled new potatoes with the salad.

Serves 4

1 cucumber
salt and pepper
225 g/8 oz fine green beans
6 eggs, hard-boiled (hard-cooked), shelled and chopped
bunch of chives, finely snipped
2 dressed crabs

Watercress Dressing

50 g/2 oz watercress
½ teaspoon sugar
1 tablespoon lemon juice
2 tablespoons olive oil
4 tablespoons plain yogurt

Trim the cucumber, remove about half the peel in fine, narrow strips and then slice it finely. Spread out the slices on a plate, season them lightly with salt and set aside for 30 minutes.

Blanch the green beans in boiling salted water for 2 minutes. Drain immediately and rinse under cold water, then drain again. Drain off the water that seeps from the cucumber and mop the slices with paper towels. Arrange the cucumber and green beans on a serving platter or individual plates. Top with the chopped eggs, sprinkle with the chives and add the crab meat.

For the dressing, finely chop the watercress and mix it with the sugar and a little seasoning. Add the lemon juice and stir until the sugar has dissolved. Then whisk in the olive oil, followed by the yogurt. Taste the dressing for seasoning before drizzling it over the salad.